Motivational Interviewing in Corrections: A Comprehensive Guide to Implementing MI in Corrections

National Institute of Corrections: U.S. Department of Justice, Bogue Bradford, Anjali Nandi

U.S. Department of Justice

National Institute of Corrections

MOTIVATIONAL INTERVIEWING IN CORRECTIONS

A Comprehensive Guide to Implementing MI in Corrections

National Institute of Corrections

U.S. Department of Justice
National Institute of Corrections
320 First Street, NW
Washington, DC 20534

Morris L. Thigpen
Director

Thomas J. Beauclair
Deputy Director

Robert Brown
Chief, Academy Division

Michael Guevara
Project Manager

National Institute of Corrections
www.nicic.gov

MOTIVATIONAL INTERVIEWING IN CORRECTIONS

A Comprehensive Guide to Implementing MI in Corrections

Bradford Bogue
Anjali Nandi

February 2012
NIC Accession Number
025556

This document was prepared under cooperative agreement number 07C70GJS5 from the National Institute of Corrections, U.S. Department of Justice. Points of view or opinions stated in this document are those of the authors and do not necessarily represent the official position or policies of the U.S. Department of Justice.

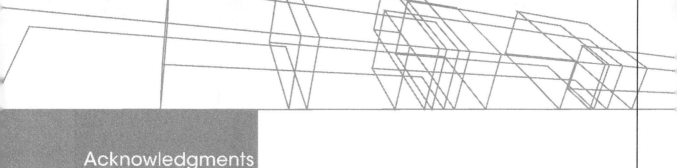

Acknowledgments

The authors wish to recognize and express our appreciation for several sources of support and guidance that enabled us to write this book. First, the creators of motivational interviewing (MI), William Miller and Stephen Rollnick, whose work continues to illuminate and inspire us in so many ways. Second, the ongoing community of practice within the Motivational Interviewing Network of Trainers provided us continual practical guidance and humility; there are so many gifted people who are learning, sharing, and training MI that it is an honor to be a part of this group. Finally, the National Institute of Corrections (NIC) and the steering group listed below provided constant support for this project. These individuals reviewed innumerable draft chapters and first-cut videos to give us extremely helpful feedback at various points throughout the development of this document.

Motivational Interviewing in Corrections: A Comprehensive Guide to Implementing MI in Corrections

NIC Steering Group

Melissa Alexander, Ph.D.	Ray Gingerich
Bryan D. Bell	Ali Hall
David Bonaiuto	Lisa Hansen
Gary Christensen, Ph.D.	Terry Marshall
Brian Coco	William R. Miller, Ph.D.
Gene Cotter	John Morris
Elizabeth Craig	Michele A. Packard, Ph.D.
Avani Gudrun Dilger	Alma Villalobos
Carl Åke Farbring	Scott T. Walters, Ph.D.
Cynthia Fix	Carl Wicklund
Matthew Gaskell	Wilburn C. (Dub) Wright

CONTENTS

CHAPTER 1 What Is Motivational Interviewing?

Motivational Interviewing (MI) is a style of communicating that helps people explore and resolve ambivalence about changing specific, maladaptive behaviors. Created by two preeminent social scientists, William Miller and Stephen Rollnick, this style is both *directive*—guided by the agent* toward specific behavior change—and client centered—attentive to the client's needs, wishes, expertise about himself/herself, and beliefs about the change process. Extensive research shows that applications of MI can be effective in assisting various client populations with challenging problems related to alcohol, methamphetamines, cocaine, opioids, sex offending, institutional conduct, and treatment compliance.[1–8]

MI can be implemented in two fundamentally different ways. First, it can be used as a general approach for working with clients, where specific skills associated with MI augment agents' supervision or communication skills. This is particularly useful when clients bring up *ambivalence* about behavior change. For example, an agent might gather better information during an assessment by increasing the use of *reflections,* an MI skill helpful in lowering client defensiveness. In discussing a positive urine test, the agent might encourage the client to describe the positive and negative aspects of drug use to explore the client's ambivalence about quitting.

MI can also be employed as a formal intervention consisting of one or several sessions to increase a person's motivation to engage in treatment. In this regard, it may be used to gather more accurate information before and after an assessment. For example, one may sandwich a client's assessment and subsequent feedback from the assessment with deliberately structured MI sessions.[9] Furthermore, making an effort to have an open conversation with the client initially about his/her hopes and concerns regarding the ensuing supervision process can often decrease defensiveness and pave the way to a very good working alliance. Following up assessment and feedback with intentional efforts to build commitment around emerging change goals helps clients clarify their own goals and, possibly, find better reasons for complying with probation.

Although agents tend to use general applications of MI more often than formal ones, over 170 of the *randomized clinical trials* (RCTs) that have been published on MI have understandably focused on MI as a brief formal intervention.[10–15]

A Brief History of Motivational Interviewing

MI emerged in the 1980s as an alternative to a counseling style largely characterized by confrontation and polarization between clients and agents—a style that had become pervasive in the addictions treatment field, particularly in the United States. Treatment research progressively indicated that this presupposing and domineering

---

*This guide uses the terms "agent" or "change agent" to refer to those professionals who counsel, treat, or otherwise assist offenders in the rehabilitation and reentry processes. The terms refer to such occupations as clinicians, counselors, outreach workers, and probation officers and are used to denote the myriad professionals who assist offenders but are too numerous to mention individually here. Those they serve—consumers of the justice system, sometimes referred to as defendants, inmates, offenders—are referred to as "clients."

approach was less than effective, but there was no clear alternative until rigorous **RCT research** on the effectiveness of MI applications began to appear.

Research that focused initially on MI applications for populations with alcohol-related problems soon broadened to consider other drug use and addictive behaviors. Several factors appear to have accelerated the transfer of MI as an innovation. The brief nature of formal MI interventions made it a good candidate for rigorous RCT research. Quality research teams initiated this research and were able to publish studies in a variety of international journals. The cost effectiveness of MI as a brief intervention also made it attractive for policy consideration.

Beginning in the late 1980s, investigations of MI applications for an ever-widening array of addiction behaviors showed similar significant effect sizes overall. (An effect size is the correlative strength between two variables, i.e., the intervention and the outcome of most interest.) This generated further interest in MI as an intervention for a wide range of health problems for which MI was not originally envisioned. This interest translated into further research on applications of MI to specific health-related behaviors (e.g., exercise for renal patients or changing unsafe sex habits), and MI applications continued to produce significantly different and better effect sizes than did control conditions.[16–18]

Following the successful innovation and application of MI in the addictions and healthcare fields, corrections systems worldwide are now beginning to implement MI. However, there are still many challenges ahead and much effort will be required to allow corrections to become the third human service field to establish MI successfully.

One of these challenges is the comparative lack of research on MI with criminal justice populations.

As a formal intervention, MI is now internationally recognized as an **evidence-based practice** (EBP) intervention for alcohol and drug problems and a wide variety of other health problems (e.g., obesity, unsafe sex, and health regimes for medical recovery). Although more recent investigations[19–21] of MI identify some of the mechanisms or causal ingredients of MI that produce significant and positive effects, the research on MI applications in criminal justice is currently insufficient to qualify MI as an EBP for offender populations. Until more corrections-specific research on MI is conducted, it is not possible to draw conclusions comparing MI to **cognitive-behavioral treatments** (CBT) and other established criminal justice EBPs in terms of recidivism reduction. Additional research is also needed regarding the level of fidelity and quality assurance in MI implementation required to produce desired client outcomes. These issues will be discussed in chapter 3.

Where Can Motivational Interviewing Fit Into Corrections?

From intake to case planning, monitoring, and sanctioning to the final case termination and transition, agents can appropriately use MI skills at almost every point in the process of correctional case management. The section below describes several applications that apply to a variety of settings and stages of supervision.

Information Gathering

Presentence investigations, intake summaries, periodic assessments, case planning, and many other routine corrections tasks rely on an agent's ability to gather accurate information from clients. In general, people disclose information more freely and accurately when they feel they are being listened to, respected, and supported. The active listening skills of MI—open questions, affirmations, reflections, and summaries (OARS)— help agents create an interpersonal environment that reduces client defensiveness and increases the quality of information gathered.[22, 23] Since this information is often used to determine supervision levels, types of treatment, and other factors, MI may also improve accuracy when it is used to assign services to clients. It may further improve the efficacy of the programs and procedures dependent on initial information gathering.

Reducing Client Resistance

Correctional settings inherently involve the use of coercive power and authority, dynamics that tend to increase client defensiveness and resistance, which can lead to both subtle and obvious conflicts with corrections staff. Staff can either increase or reduce this potential for conflict depending on the way they approach clients. While a certain amount of control and directness are necessary in effectively managing client populations, approaches that go beyond this and attempt to actively persuade or threaten clients into changing require considerable time and energy and tend to be ineffective in the long term.

Successful MI implementation involves replacing authoritarian and advocacy approaches with MI techniques.[24–28] These techniques may include reflecting, rather than reacting to, resistant statements, helping clients improve communication effectiveness by providing them with feedback about perceived resistance, and exploring clients' natural ambivalence about changing their behavior. These techniques lay the foundation from which agents can build a collaborative *working alliance*[29–31] with clients. In line with the findings from psychology, applied criminology researchers have determined that the staff-client relationship is paramount. The second principle of the *eight principles of evidence-based practice* in community corrections[32] suggests that using communication strategies that value a client's perspectives helps build a working relationship with that client and provides a practical and valuable alternative to escalating the use of authority and control.[33, 34] MI interventions have proven particularly effective with clients who are angry[35]

or in the early stages of motivation to change.[36, 37] These are the very clients who require the most coercion and persuasion when using control and advocacy approaches.

Providing a Structure for Advancing Behavior Change

Even the most motivated people can find change to be an uneven process. As clients cycle between high and low levels of motivation, staff need to be able to recognize and respond to these stages with interactions that will facilitate rather than impede movement toward change. Staff may improve their routine interactions with clients by using MI strategies for identifying clients' current stance toward change and responding in ways that have proven effective in similar cases. By providing an overarching set of principles to refer to, the MI approach can make it easier for an agent to help guide the change process, linking routine interpersonal interactions to agency and case objectives.

MI's focus on eliciting client motivation to change can also help agents prioritize a client's criminogenic needs. Many high-risk clients have multiple criminogenic needs, requiring them to change more than one target behavior at any time. One way to prioritize these needs is for staff to use MI's active listening skills to determine which behaviors the client is most motivated to change at a particular time. Staff can then prioritize client behaviors and target them accordingly for further discussion about the client's ambivalence about making changes.

As clients feel supported by a working alliance with staff, and as they have the chance to resolve more of their ambivalence about behavior change, the MI approach helps staff identify and strengthen areas in which clients are motivated. Staff can use MI to draw out clients' statements expressing their desire, ability, reasons, need, and commitment to making particular changes. It is the latter client self-motivating statements that are predictive of long-term target behavior change.

Preventing Burnout

Burnout, or emotional exhaustion, is common for staff who have been inadequately trained in purposeful and effective strategies for working with high-risk, challenging, unwilling clients.[38–40] Burnout may be summarized by the old corrections saying, "The first year we did everything we could for them, the second year we did everything we could to them, and the third year we just didn't care." What is exhausting in this saying is the implication that all the effort is on the side of the staff person who must "do for" and "do to" the client.

> Moving outside of the immediate staff-client relationship, applications of MI can also help improve organizational culture and morale.

Using MI skills, rather than advocacy and control methods, can empower agents to engage difficult clients in an interesting, proactive manner that continues to highlight the prosocial contribution of corrections work. The burden of forcing resistant people to change may be transformed into the creative challenge of identifying and drawing out where people are already motivated. When MI techniques are able to facilitate a collaborative working alliance, rather than a combative control struggle, the client and staff are able to work together. As the burden for change is now shared, resulting behavior changes can be motivating for both the client and the agent, reducing the feeling of ineffectiveness and struggle that leads to staff burnout.[41]

Humanizing the Corrections Paradigm

Moving outside of the immediate staff-client relationship, applications of MI can also help improve *organizational culture* and morale. Fundamentally, MI is about having respect for people's inherent autonomy, caring for their well-being, and being willing to collaborate and form partnerships for the ensuing change and support enterprise. All of the techniques of MI flow from this respectful, collaborative spirit that can help temper, humanize, and shift the corrections paradigm, one that currently tends to be autocratic with a "command and control" focus.

Shifting the way staff work with clients can also translate to a shift in the way staff interact with each other. As corrections staff practice this way of being, they model it to their clients, and the spirit spills over into staff interactions and shared agency values and orientations.[42]

In addition to spontaneous changes in staff interactions that tend to occur as people practice MI, a more intentional transformation of organizational climate may also be pursued through the creation of MI *communities of practice*—groups of individuals who meet regularly to provide each other practice opportunities and feedback over a set period of time. Current research on implementation in human services[43–46] and more specific research on MI training and implementation[47–53] suggests that even the best training workshop can only help trainees *learn* about MI. Implementing MI on the job after training requires followup strategies of providing trainees with (1) objective feedback of their MI performance and (2) skill coaching or guided practice.[49, 51] These key posttraining strategies may be provided by the creation of formal or informal communities of practice.

Communities of practice are parallel learning organizations and can be very empowering,[46, 56–58] as they have been in the past for the addictions treatment field. Coworkers are rarely given the opportunity to be open with each other about their skill limitations and progress. Yet, as staff become accustomed to practicing with each other and collaborating toward the goal of better skill acquisition, organizational culture norms tend to shift as well. Privacy, isolation, and the rigid protection of status quo approaches of interacting with clients can gradually give way to shared values of open dialogue, partnership, and a willingness to try new approaches that might improve client outcomes. The resulting increases in collaboration and feelings of interpersonal effectiveness can help staff feel supported and valued in their efforts to work together—within and outside of their immediate organization—to bring about positive changes in the lives of clients and, consequently, in the greater community.

Even though each of the above applications of MI in corrections offers potential benefits in terms of staff morale, staff-client interactions, case management, and client outcomes, there are significant implementation challenges that corrections agencies must overcome to reap the full benefits of MI strategies. This manual provides guidelines for bridging the gap between status quo agency procedures and effective MI implementation. The remaining section of this chapter explains how this manual and mixed-media package may assist different levels of corrections agents in adapting MI for the purposes described above.

Organization and Design of This Guide

As a companion document to the National Institute of Corrections' (NIC's) monograph *Motivating Offenders to Change*,[24] this manual serves as a reference guide for implementing MI in correctional settings. *Motivating Offenders to Change* introduces MI applications in corrections and serves as a primer for developing MI skills in corrections; *Motivational Interviewing in Corrections* provides descriptive materials, information, and tools for supporting implementation of MI in correctional settings. To reap the maximum benefit from this reference tool, it is important to understand how it is organized.

Motivational Interviewing is divided into two books—*Motivational Interviewing in Corrections: A Comprehensive Guide to Implementing MI in Corrections* (book I) and *Exercises for Developing MI Skills in Corrections* (book II). The first four chapters of book I, *Motivational Interviewing in Corrections,* address background and fundamental issues related to agency or systemwide implementation of MI:

Chapter 1: What Is Motivational Interviewing?—Presents a brief history of MI, how it fits in corrections, and how it is presented in this book.

Chapter 2: How Motivational Interviewing Is Learned—Describes eight integral stages or tasks for learning MI.

Chapter 3: Supervising and Coaching To Support Implementation—Outlines four roles or mechanisms for promoting and supporting staff MI skills after training:

- Firstline supervisor duties.

- Coaching MI.

- *Clinical supervision.*

- Quality assurance.

Chapter 4: Assessing Motivational Interviewing Skills—Provides an overview of basic tactics for assessing MI skill use, providing a basis for feedback, coaching, quality assurance, and research.

Chapter 5: Planning To Help Individuals Develop MI Skills in a Correctional Setting—Guides readers through the steps of implementation and sustaining MI in the workplace.

Although staff may *learn about* MI from a 1- to 3-day workshop, acquiring the capacity to *use* MI in on-the-job settings requires several posttraining followup strategies.[49, 51] These chapters clarify the processes required for staff to learn and implement MI on an ongoing basis.

The final chapters of *Motivational Interviewing in Corrections* address agency issues, such as organizational norms, mental models, and leadership styles that can significantly affect the success of MI implementation. These chapters highlight strategic opportunities for implementing MI on a larger scale beyond training and coaching, and aligning routine operational processes to better accommodate and support MI. They also help build a research agenda for empirically testing various MI applications. These issues will likely be of interest to management, trainers, and coaches, but not necessarily to line staff.

Book II, *Exercises for Developing MI Skills in Corrections*, links Miller and Moyers' **eight tasks for learning MI** [59, 60] (see chapter 2 of book I) to scenarios that agents commonly encounter in their efforts to monitor and reinforce court/parole/institutional conditions and address clients' **central eight criminogenic needs**.[58, 59] This book also considers the learning tasks of MI in relation to the **eight principles for effective interventions** outlined in *Implementing Evidence-Based Practice in Community Corrections: The Principles of Effective Intervention*, an NIC publication.[32] Ordered in the sequence in which they are most commonly learned or mastered, the first five of these eight tasks for learning MI provide the structure for *Exercises for Developing MI Skills in Corrections*. Each chapter corresponds to an MI learning task:

Chapter 1: The Spirit of Motivational Interviewing—Outlines how to work with clients in collaborative relationships, evoke clients' internal motivation to change, and support clients' autonomy in choosing positive changes.

Chapter 2: Active Listening—Provides an overview of responding to and directing clients with open questions, affirmations, reflections, and summarizations (OARS).

Chapter 3: Recognizing and Reinforcing Change Talk—Helps agents notice when clients make statements indicating an inclination to move toward change and helps agents help clients strengthen the statements they make supporting change.

Chapter 4: Eliciting and Strengthening Change Talk—Helps agents understand how to magnify clients' existing momentum for change and help clients move from ambivalence about change to commitment to change.

Chapter 5: Responding to Resistance—Focuses on reflecting and providing helpful feedback about client resistance to change or to change agents, rather than responding with a reactionary power struggle.

These chapters are organized so that resources most relevant to addressing MI needs and work contexts are readily accessible. Each chapter begins with a description of the skills and performance challenges related to that chapter's MI learning task, followed by a description of ways that the learning task can be fulfilled in the context of monitoring and reinforcing terms and conditions across the central eight criminogenic needs.

The final part of each chapter describes how the relevant MI "skill set" relates to agent roles and functions outlined in the eight principles for effective intervention or evidence-based practice. Each chapter is accompanied by a DVD containing examples, teaching aids, and other tools that support skill development.

Thus, *Exercises for Developing MI Skills in Corrections* organizes the various MI resources in each chapter by relating them to the following three sets of principles, in this order:

THE CENTRAL EIGHT CRIMINOGENIC NEEDS

1. Current Dysfunctional Family Relations
2. Antisocial Peer Relations
3. Recreation/Leisure Problems
4. Employment/Education Problems
5. Alcohol and Other Drug Problems
6. History of Antisocial Behavior Associated with Low Self-Control Problems
7. Antisocial Beliefs/Attitudes
8. Criminal Personality Features

1. The eight tasks for learning MI.

2. The common terms, conditions, and central eight criminogenic need areas that agents generally spend time monitoring and reinforcing.

3. The eight guiding principles for EBP in corrections.

Understanding how the principles relate to one another will facilitate the effective use of the wide variety of specific information, tools, and video scenarios that accompany these books. The following two examples illustrate how the chapter structure in *Exercises for Developing MI Skills in Corrections* works and how using the accompanying resources may enhance one's learning of MI:

Example 1. Alan, an agent who recently attended an introductory training, is unclear about the difference between complex and simple reflections and feels uncertain about his use of these skills. He decides that he needs to focus on the active listening skills of reflections, affirmations, open questions, and summaries—the "using active listening skills" learning task of MI—to further develop MI proficiency. Alan knows that his next two scheduled supervision contacts are with clients whose criminogenic need priorities are substance abuse and antisocial peers. To prepare to use active listening skills in these upcoming meetings, Alan turns to *Exercises for Developing MI Skills in Corrections,* chapter 2: "Active Listening" and looks through examples on the use of active listening with clients with these criminogenic needs. He looks first at the topic overview at the beginning of the chapter to compare the descriptions of simple and complex reflections. Then

---

EIGHT PRINCIPLES FOR EFFECTIVE INTERVENTION OR EVIDENCE-BASED PRACTICE

1. Using valid assessments for risk of recidivism and criminogenic needs.

2. Engaging clients in a manner that promotes **intrinsic motivation** and a favorable working alliance.

3. Targeting interventions and case priorities according to the risk, need, and responsivity principles derived from meta-analysis of client interventions.

4. Emphasizing cognitive-behavioral treatment whenever providing programming.

5. Increasing the systematic (i.e., immediate, certain) application of reinforcements for behavior, especially positive reinforcements for exhibiting desired behavior.

6. Mobilizing a variety of mechanisms for improving **social support** within a person's natural community.

7. Measuring, monitoring, and assessing relevant behavior performance, skills, and practices.

8. Providing objective feedback on performance.

Source: Adapted from B. Bogue, N. Campbell, M. Carey, E. Clawson, D. Faust, K. Florio, L. Joplin, G. Keiser, B. Wasson, and W. Woodward, *Implementing Evidence-Based Practice in Community Corrections: The Principles of Effective Intervention* (Washington, DC: U.S. Department of Justice, National Institute of Corrections, 2004), www.nicic.gov/pubs/2004/019342. pdf.

Alan finds both transcribed dialogues and video scenarios providing the examples he needs. After reviewing them, he views the tool DVD and practices the written exercise game designed to help agents differentiate between simple and complex reflections.

Example 2. Yolanda, a supervisor, MI coach, and trainer, wants to know how MI might apply to the rollout of a new assessment instrument. She knows some staff have never been trained in MI and others have received a series of trainings interspersed with coaching. She decides to contact the people who have been coaching the agents and determines that most participating agents are currently working on skills for dealing with client resistance. Yolanda now has several different avenues for getting prepared. To begin working with staff who have not yet been trained in MI, she reviews *Exercises for Developing MI Skills in Corrections,* chapter 1: "The Spirit of MI"—the logical starting point for learning MI. She specifically reviews the information on how the

MI spirit fits into and enhances assessment (EBP principle 1). For the staff who have already been trained, Yolanda turns to chapter 5: "Responding to Resistance." She finds tools and aids in that chapter where EBP principles 1 and 2, assessment and developing working alliances, respectively, are discussed. She also looks at more specific situations for dealing with resistance under each of the criminogenic areas.

Endnotes

1. A.L. Stotts, J.M. Schmitz, H.M. Rhoades, and J. Grabowski, "Motivational Interviewing With Cocaine-Dependent Patients: A Pilot Study," *Journal of Consulting and Clinical Psychology* 69(5):858–62, 2001.

2. B. Saunders, C. Wilkinson, and M. Phillips, "The Impact of a Brief Motivational Intervention With Opiate Users Attending a Methadone Programme," *Addiction* 90(3):415–24, 1995.

3. F.J. Porporino, D. Robinson, B. Millson, and J.R. Weekes, "An Outcome Evaluation of Prison-Based Treatment Programming for Substance Users," *Substance Use and Misuse* 37(8–10):1047, 2002.

4. W.R. Miller, C.E. Yahne, and J.S. Tonigan, "Motivational Interviewing in Drug Abuse Services: A Randomized Trial," *Journal of Consulting and Clinical Psychology* 71(4):754–63, 2003.

5. J.I. Ginsburg, R.E. Mann, F. Rotgers, and J.R. Weekes, "Motivational Interviewing With Criminal Justice Populations," in W.R. Miller and S.R. Rollnick (eds.), *Motivational Interviewing: Preparing People for Change*, 2d ed. (New York: Guilford Press, 2002), pp. 333–46.

6. R.J. Garland and M.J. Dougher, "Motivational Intervention in the Treatment of Sex Offenders," in W.R. Miller and S.R. Rollnick (eds.), *Motivational Interviewing: Preparing People To Change Addictive Behavior* (New York: Guilford Press, 1991), pp. 303–13.

7. K.M. Carroll, S.A. Ball, C. Nich, S. Martino, T.L. Frankforter, C. Farentinos, L.E. Kunkel, S.K. Mikulich-Gilbertson, J. Morgenstern, J.L. Obert, D. Polcin, N. Snead, and G.E. Woody, "Motivational Interviewing To Improve Treatment Engagement and Outcome in Individuals Seeking Treatment for Substance Abuse: A Multisite Effectiveness Study," *Drug and Alcohol Dependence* 81(3):301–12, 2006.

8. J.M. Brown and W.R. Miller, "Impact of Motivational Interviewing on Participation and Outcome in Residential Alcoholism Treatment," *Psychology of Addictive Behaviors* 7(4):211–18, 1993.

9. S. Martino, S.A. Ball, S.L. Gallon, D. Hall, M. Garcia, S. Ceperich, C. Farentinos, J. Hamilton, and W. Hausotter, *Motivational Interviewing Assessment: Supervisory Tools for Enhancing Proficiency* (Salem, OR: Northwest Frontier Addiction Technology Transfer Center, Oregon Health and Science University, 2006).

10. E.I. Vasilaki, S.G. Hosier, and W.M. Cox, "The Efficacy of Motivational Interviewing as a Brief Intervention for Excessive Drinking: A Meta-Analytic Review," *Alcohol and Alcoholism* 41(3):328–35, 2006.

11. S. Rubak, A. Sandboek, T. Lauritzen, and B. Christensen, "Motivational Interviewing: A Systematic Review and Meta-Analysis," *British Journal of General Practice* 55(513):305–12, 2005.

12. A. Moyer and J. Finney, "Brief Interventions for Alcohol Problems: Factors That Facilitate Implementation," *Alcohol Research and Health* 28(1):44–50, 2004/2005.

13. J. McCambridge and J. Strang, "The Efficacy of Single-Session Motivational Interviewing in Reducing Drug Consumption and Perceptions of Drug-Related Risk and Harm Among Young People: Results From a Multi-Site Cluster Randomized Trial," *Addiction* 99(1):39–52, 2004.

14. B.L. Burke, H. Arkowitz, and C. Dunn, "The Efficacy of Motivational Interviewing and Its Adaptations: What We Know So Far," in W.R. Miller and S.R. Rollnick (eds.), *Motivational Interviewing: Preparing People for Change*, 2d ed. (New York: Guilford Press, 2002), pp. 217–50.

15. T.H. Bien, W.R. Miller, and J.S. Tonigan, "Brief Interventions for Alcohol Problems: A Review," *Addiction* 88(3):315–35, 1993.

16. K. Emmons and S. Rollnick, "Motivational Interviewing in Health Care Settings: Opportunities and Limitations," *American Journal of Preventative Medicine* 20(1):68–74, 2001.

17. S. Butterworth, A. Linden, W. McClay, and M.C. Leo, "Effect of Motivational Interviewing-Based Health Coaching on Employees' Physical and Mental Health Status," *Journal of Occupational Health Psychology* 11(4):358–65, 2006.

18. K. Bell and T. Tanabe, Motivational interviewing: How to improve your success in promoting health behavior change. Unpublished manuscript, 2005.

19. T.B. Moyers, W.R. Miller, and S.M.L. Hendrickson, "How Does Motivational Interviewing Work? Therapist Interpersonal Skill Predicts Client Involvement Within Motivational Interviewing Sessions," *Journal of Consulting and Clinical Psychology* 73(4):590–98, 2005.

20. P.C. Amrhein, "How Does Motivational Interviewing Work? What Client Talk Reveals," *Journal of Cognitive Psychotherapy* 18(4):323–36, 2004.

21. T.B. Moyers, T. Martin, P.J. Christopher, J.M. Houck, J.S. Tonigan, and P.C. Amrhein, "Client Language as a Mediator of Motivational Interviewing Efficacy: Where Is the Evidence?" *Alcoholism—Clinical and Experimental Research* 31(Suppl. 10):40S–47S, 2007.

22. T.B. Moyers and T. Martin, "Therapist Influence on Client Language During Motivational Interviewing Sessions," *Journal of Substance Abuse Treatment* 30(3):245–51, 2006.

23. D. Catley, K.J. Harris, M.S. Mayo, S. Hall, K.S. Okuyemi, T. Boardman, and J.S. Ahluwalia, "Adherence to Principles of Motivational Interviewing and Client Within-Session Behavior," *Behavioural and Cognitive Psychotherapy* 34(1):43–56, 2006.

24. S.T. Walters, M.D. Clark, R. Gingerich, and M.L. Meltzer, *Motivating Offenders to Change: A Guide for Probation and Parole* (Washington, DC: U.S. Department of Justice, National Institute of Corrections, 2007).

25. C. Reddick, "Motivational Interviewing of Offenders," in E.R. Walsh (ed.), *Community Corrections Report* (Fitchburg, MA, 2002), pp. 42–45.

26. W. Miller, "Pros and Cons: Reflections on Motivational Interviewing in Correctional Settings," *Motivational Interviewing Newsletter: Updates, Education and Training* 6(1):2–3, 1999.

27. M.D. Clark, "Motivational Interviewing for Probation Officers: Tipping the Balance Toward Change," *Federal Probation* 7(1):38–44, 2006.

28. A. Brickner, P. Hofmann, M. Packard, and D. Stein, *Setting the Stage for Change: The Use of Motivational Interviewing with Offenders* (Denver, CO: Colorado Department of Public Safety, 1996).

29. J.C. Norcross, *Psychotherapy Relationships That Work* (New York: Oxford University Press, 2002).

30. M.J. Lambert and D.E. Barley, "Research Summary on the Therapeutic Relationship and Psychotherapy Outcome," in J. Norcross (ed.), *Psychotherapy Relationships That Work.*

Therapist Contributions and Responsiveness to Patients (London, England: Oxford University Press, 2002), pp. 17–28.

31. A.O. Horvath, "The Alliance in Context: Accomplishments, Challenges, and Future Directions," *Psychotherapy: Theory, Research, Practice, Training* 43(3):258–63, 2006.

32. B. Bogue, N. Campbell, M. Carey, E. Clawson, D. Faust, K. Florio, L. Joplin, G. Keiser, B. Wasson, and W. Woodward, *Implementing Evidence-Based Practice in Community Corrections: The Principles of Effective Intervention* (Washington, DC: U.S. Department of Justice, National Institute of Corrections, 2004).

33. T. Palmer, "Programmatic and Nonprogrammatic Aspects to Successful Intervention: New Directions for Research," *Crime and Delinquency* 41(1):100–31, 1995.

34. C. Dowden and D. Andrews, "The Importance of Staff Practice Delivering Effective Correctional Treatment: A Meta-Analytic Review of Core Correctional Practice," *International Journal of Offender Therapy and Comparative Criminology* 48(2):203–14, 2004.

35. Project MATCH Research Group, "Matching Patients With Alcohol Disorders to Treatments: Clinical Implications From Project MATCH," *Journal of Mental Health* 7(6):589–602, 1998.

36. S. Rollnick, N. Heather, A. Bell, and R. Richmond, Matching excessive drinkers to brief interventions by readiness to change: Brief motivational interviewing versus skills-based counseling. Unpublished article, Australian Commonwealth Department of Health, Housing, Local Government and Community Services, 1994.

37. W.R. Miller and S. Rollnick, "Talking Oneself Into Change: Motivational Interviewing, Stages of Change, and Therapeutic Process," *Journal of Cognitive Psychotherapy* 18(4):299–308, 2004.

38. J.T. Whitehead and C.A. Lindquist, "Job Stress and Burnout Among Probation/Parole Officers: Perceptions and Causal Factors," *International Journal of Offender Therapy and Comparative Criminology* 29(2):109–19, 1985.

39. R.N. Slate, W.W. Johnson, and T.L. Wells, "Probation Officer Stress: Is There an Organizational Cure?" *Federal Probation* 64(1):56–59, 2000.

40. P. Finn, *Addressing Correctional Officer Stress: Programs and Strategies* (Washington, DC: U.S. Department of Justice, Office of Justice Programs, National Institute of Justice, 2000).

41. J.T. Whitehead, *Burnout in Probation and Corrections* (New York: Praeger Publishers, 1989), p. 159.

42. K.S. Cameron, J.E. Dutton, and R.E. Quinn (eds.), *Positive Organizational Scholarship: Foundations of a New Discipline* (San Francisco: Berrett-Koehler Publishers, 2003), p. 465.

43. S. Nutley, H. Davies, and I. Walter, Evidence based policy and practice: Cross sector lessons from the UK. Paper presented at the Social Policy Research and Evaluation Conference, Wellington, New Zealand, 2002, *www.ruru.ac.uk/PDFs/NZ%20conference%20 paper%20final%20170602.pdf.*

44. D. Fixsen, S.F. Naoom, K.A. Blase, R.M. Friedman, and F. Wallace, *Implementation Research: A Synthesis of the Literature* (Tampa, FL: University of South Florida, Louis de la Parte Florida Mental Health Institute, The National Implementation Research Network, 2005).

45. P. Ellickson, J. Petersilia, M. Caggiano, and S. Polin, *Implementing New Ideas in Criminal Justice* (Santa Monica, CA: RAND Corporation, 1983).

46. P.W. Corrigan, L. Steiner, S.G. McCracken, B. Blaser, and M. Barr, "Strategies for Disseminating Evidence-Based Practices to Staff Who Treat People With Serious Mental Illness," *Psychiatric Services* 52(12):1598–1606, 2001.

47. C.E. Yahne, W.R. Miller, T.B. Moyers, and M. Pirritanno, *Teaching Motivational Interviewing to Clinicians: A Randomized Trial of Training Methods* (Albuquerque, NM: Center on Alcoholism, Substance Abuse, and Addictions, 2004).

48. E.P. Schoener, C.L. Madeja, M.J. Henderson, S.J. Ondersma, and J.J. Janisse, "Effects of Motivational Interviewing Training on Mental Health Therapist Behavior," *Drug and Alcohol Dependence* 82(3):269–75, 2006.

49. T.B. Moyers, T. Martin, J.K. Manuel, S. Hendrickson, and W.R. Miller, "Assessing Competence in the Use of Motivational Interviewing," *Journal of Substance Abuse Treatment* 28(1):19–26, 2005.

50. W.R. Miller, C.E. Yahne, T.B. Moyers, J. Martinez, and M. Pirritanno, "A Randomized Trial of Methods to Help Clinicians Learn Motivational Interviewing," *Journal of Consulting and Clinical Psychology* 72(6):1050–62, 2004.

51. W.R. Miller and K.A. Mount, "A Small Study of Training in Motivational Interviewing: Does One Workshop Change Clinician and Client Behavior?" *Behavioural and Cognitive Psychotherapy* 29(4):457–71, 2001.

52. G. Corbett, "What the Research Says...About MI Training," *MINT Bulletin* 13(1):12–14, 2006.

53. J.S. Baer, D.R. Kivlahan, and D.M. Donovan, "Integrating Skills Training and Motivational Therapies: Implications for the Treatment of Substance Dependence," *Journal of Substance Abuse Treatment* 17(1–2):15–23, 1999.

54. E. Sauve, "Informal Knowledge Transfer," *Training and Development* 61(3):22–24, 2007.

55. C.D. Norman and T. Huerta, "Knowledge Transfer and Exchange Through Social Networks: Building Foundations for a Community of Practice Within Tobacco Control," *Implementation Science* 1(20), 2006.

56. E.L. Lesser and J. Storck, "Communities of Practice and Organizational Performance," *IBM Systems Journal* 40(4):6, 2001.

57. T.B. Moyers and W.R. Miller, "Eight Stages in Learning Motivational Interviewing," *Journal of Teaching in the Addictions* 5(1):15, 2006.

58. W.R. Miller and T.B. Moyers, Eight stages in learning motivational interviewing. Unpublished research article, University of New Mexico, 2004.

59. J. Bonta and D.A. Andrews, *Risk-Need-Responsivity Model for Offender Assessment and Rehabilitation* (Ottowa, Ontario, Canada: Carleton University, 2007).

60. D.A. Andrews, C. Dowden, and P. Gendreau, Clinically relevant and psychologically informed approaches to reduced re-offending: A meta-analytic study of human service, risk, need, responsivity, and other concerns in justice contexts. Unpublished manuscript, Ottawa, Ontario, Canada, 1999.

CHAPTER 2 How Motivational Interviewing Is Learned

The efficacy of motivational interviewing (MI) has been studied extensively with heartening results; there have been close to 200 randomized clinical trials (RTCs) conducted on MI. Most of these studies show significant direct effects or benefits of MI as compared to control conditions, specifically in the areas of treatment **engagement** and **retention** in a variety of fields related to behavior change, including addictions and health. A number of quality meta-analyses summarize both the research and relative effect sizes across different populations.[1–4] Today, the focus of research on MI is shifting to examine its transfer and implementation. This includes questions about whether the current method of training agents on MI (a 2- to 3-day workshop) is sufficient to acquire MI skills, how supervisors know whether agents who say they are using MI are actually doing so, and how agents maintain MI skills to a degree sufficient to affect client responses and progress.

Motivational interviewing is a style of evoking change that includes a spirit, or way of interacting (e.g., collaborative, evocative, and respecting autonomy), and the use of specific skills (e.g., asking open questions, listening reflectively, eliciting and reinforcing change talk) to explore and help clients resolve their ambivalence toward making behavior change. As an individual's ambivalence regarding change declines, there are more opportunities for the person to build intrinsic motivation and commitment to change.

Certain agent behaviors, such as persuading, arguing, and directing rather than listening, are inconsistent with MI. Implementing MI is not just about using new skills, but changing (or eliminating) old ones that are ineffective and/or inconsistent with MI. The outcomes of approaches like MI are strongly supported by research; on the other hand, approaches involving blaming, judging, and pessimism about a client's capacity to change are all related to poorer outcomes (e.g., not completing probation successfully), especially for involuntary clients.[5, 6]

Miller and Mount[7] conducted a study to gauge the effectiveness of a single workshop on probation agent behavior and resulting client responses. In this study, the researchers provided a 2-day workshop to 22 probation officers and community corrections counselors. The participants completed written questionnaires and provided a taped sample of their skills before, directly after, and 4 months following the training. The questionnaires and tapes were coded using the **Motivational Interviewing Skill Code** (MISC) system. The researchers found that agents' self-reporting of competence was not related to the skills demonstrated in the taped sessions, that the gains that agents made in acquiring MI skills were not significant enough to influence client responses, that agents tended to drift back to their old business-as-usual skills, and that although agents did acquire MI skills, they did not change prior habits of behaviors that are inconsistent with MI.

Research from the National Institute on Drug Abuse's Clinical Trials Network[8] demonstrates similar findings. The trials had a dual purpose: (1) to determine the effect that using MI during an intake session had on client retention and substance abuse, and (2) to examine the implementation of an evidence-based practice (EBP) (i.e., MI) in a real-world setting, to ensure that agents were using MI with integrity.

Study participants were 423 substance-abusing clients in 5 community-based, outpatient treatment settings. The findings demonstrated that adding MI to one intake session at the beginning of treatment increases engagement in treatment and treatment retention. The findings also showed that agent fidelity to MI can be maintained at high levels when agents are provided with effective clinical supervision that includes reviewing and coding taped sessions.[8, 9] Based on these results, it appears that to be able to use and maintain MI skills effectively, agents must not only be trained in MI, but also supported in the development and retention of their skills through regular coaching, MI-adherent supervision, and feedback received from taped sessions.[9]

Existing research on MI acquisition[10, 11] challenges the current way of providing training in MI—usually in small doses, e.g., a 2- to 3-day basic training followed by a 2- to 3-day advanced training. The driving factor for determining proficiency tends to be the amount of training a person has received. With a current understanding about MI transfer, however, it becomes clear that there is a need to focus more on training in accordance with criteria, where observation, feedback, coaching, and supervision determine (and ensure maintenance of) proficiency. In fact, *experimental/control research*[12, 13] identifies feedback and coaching as the most crucial factors in learning MI. This guide, therefore, focuses not only on providing an understanding of the spirit and skills of MI, but also emphasizes the use of coaching and supervision to maintain and improve MI skills.

Process of Learning MI

If the focus of this guide is on supporting the proficient learning of MI, then it must consider how agents learn MI and whether there are developmental tasks that agents complete in acquiring proficiency. Miller and Moyers[11] indicate that there are *eight progressive tasks* that agents

typically work on when developing competence in MI. These tasks tend to be developmental; an earlier task is likely to be requisite for later tasks. The tasks also loosely match the phases that agents support clients through—exploring ambivalence, building motivation, and building commitment to change.

Task 1. The Spirit of Motivational Interviewing. The first learning task for MI is the willingness of agents to be open to the assumptions inherent in the *spirit of MI.* Miller and Rollnick[15] have described the underlying spirit of MI as a way of being and interacting with clients that is collaborative, evocative, and conveys respect for the client's autonomy. Specifically, being collaborative means being in partnership with clients and creating an atmosphere that supports change as opposed to trying to force change. Being evocative indicates a willingness to draw motivation out of clients rather than trying to impose it. It acknowledges and conveys respect for the inherent wisdom of clients and bolsters the belief that, given supportive conditions, people tend to develop and change in a positive direction. Finally, since the goal of MI is to enhance intrinsic motivation, agents convey respect for clients' *autonomy* and communicate that the responsibility of changing lies with the client.

Often, for agents learning MI, congruence with the MI spirit comes with time and the practice of MI. The spirit of MI is the first task in learning MI, because learning MI requires openness to its spirit. This does not mean that agents have to embrace the spirit fully in the beginning, but they must be willing to suspend contrary beliefs. After all, it will become more difficult to learn and practice MI if one's assumptions about clients are antithetical to MI.

Task 2. OARS: Client-Centered Listening Skills. The next learning task for agents is proficiency with basic active listening skills, such as asking *open questions (O),* providing *affirmations (A), listening reflectively (R),* and *summarizing (S).* These skills form the basis of the first phase of MI that agents support their clients through, where agents encourage clients to explore and articulate their ambivalence. Agents gather information by using open questions, providing support, and conveying respect using affirmations. The agent then groups the information in a coherent fashion using summaries. The most challenging part of this task is expressing accurate empathy to clients by using reflections that convey an understanding of clients' words and meaning.

Being client-centered is more complex than just repeating what a client has said. It is being able to reflect something the client is feeling or experiencing but has not yet explicitly stated. Reflections convey empathy and can also serve other purposes, e.g., rolling with resistance (see below) or developing discrepancy. The basic skills, known together as OARS, form the basis for learning the next steps in MI.

Task 3. Recognizing and Reinforcing Change Talk. Motivational interviewing, while client-centered, is also a directive method where clients' responses are selectively reflected and reinforced. Psycholinguistic (psychological factors involved in language) analyses of taped MI sessions reveal a link between clients' expressed *change talk* (statements that express desire, ability, reason, need, or commitment to change) and actual behavioral change.[16] This change talk can occur naturally when a client is exploring ambivalence

and making arguments for change. MI's strategic reinforcement of these arguments for change is what differentiates it from purely client-centered methods. To be able to reinforce these arguments, agents must recognize and respond to client change talk as it naturally occurs in the exploration of ambivalence. When an agent is unable to recognize change talk, he/she may miss valuable cues about client readiness to change, along with opportunities to reinforce emerging motivation.

Task 4. Eliciting and Strengthening Change Talk. Building on the previous task of recognizing change talk as it naturally occurs, the next task is learning how to intentionally draw it out. Various methods of *eliciting change talk* are described by Miller and Rollnick[15] and will be elaborated on in *Exercises for Developing MI Skills in Corrections*. In this learning task, agents gain efficacy at not only eliciting, but also building on and strengthening change talk. Because of this link between change talk and actual behavior changes, a client's change talk statements are like pearls—gems of information that an agent must recognize and respond to, whether by asking for more pearls, reflecting them, affirming them, or gathering them in a necklace and offering them back to the client. In this way, agents learn to be strategic about what they invite clients to think about, talk about, and respond to. Care is taken to not elicit *"sustain talk,"* where clients make arguments against change. Rather, agents learn to recognize signs of readiness and begin to elicit from clients verbal momentum toward change. By believing in clients' inner resources for change and then structuring conversations through specific strategies (e.g., *querying extremes* and/or *decisional-balance work*), agents can significantly increase the probability of drawing out change talk from their clients.

Task 5. Rolling With Resistance. "Rolling with resistance" is one of the four guiding principles of motivational interviewing.[15] This

---

EIGHT TASKS FOR LEARNING MI

1. Exploring the spirit of MI.

2. Using client-centered skills (OARS).

3. Recognizing change talk.

4. Eliciting and reinforcing change talk.

5. Rolling with resistance.

6. Developing a change plan.

7. Consolidating client commitment.

8. Integrating MI with other intervention methods.

Source: W.R. Miller and T.B. Moyers, "Eight Stages in Learning Motivational Interviewing," *Journal of Teaching in the Addictions* 5(1):3–17, 2007.

learning task challenges agents to respond skillfully to resistance in a way that does not increase it but, instead, reflects it and conveys respect for it. Human beings, particularly those in the human service field, have a strong desire to help others along the right path and to fix problems.[15] This reflex, termed the *"righting reflex"* by Miller and Rollnick,[15] can cause an agent to meet client ambivalence about, or resistance to, change with passionate arguments for why the client should change and even how the client should do so. This meeting of resistance head-on usually results in the client further defending the position of not changing, thereby augmenting his/her resistance to change. In this learning task, agents begin to develop skills that help them acknowledge resistance, convey respect for it, invite new perspectives, and view the presence of resistance as an indicator that they will need to use different strategies and skills. It is possible that resistance skills are learned in this later task and not an earlier one, because more than any others, these skills are used and best practiced under "hot" conditions that are potentially stressful.

Task 6. Developing a Change Plan. The next learning task is to recognize when clients are ready to move into the next phase of MI, where commitment to a *change plan* is strengthened. Knowing when to transition becomes important because a client who is ready to prepare for change will be frustrated by an agent who continues to explore ambivalence. Likewise, a client who is not ready to prepare for change will convey resistance if the agent moves too quickly ahead of the client.

Transitioning to the next phase of MI usually involves using a transitional summary of preparatory change talk and asking a key open question that focuses on what's next. For example, "Where do we go from here?" "What do you think you will do at this point?" or "What's the next step for you?" are key open questions. The agent helps the client explore a menu of options rather than promoting just one course of action. The client is

then supported in preparing for change, and the agent can now negotiate a change plan in which the client is invested and has taken ownership. Agents must resist the inclination to take over for the client, developing a change plan for the client and thereby losing focus on the client's autonomy.

Task 7. Consolidating Client Commitment. The previous learning task involved the agent recognizing readiness for and supporting the client in preparing for change. This seventh learning task is about developing skillfulness in consolidating a client's commitment to change into a workable plan. The talk that agents look for from a client is more about "I will" rather than "I want to." Moyers et al.[14] stress the importance of supporting the client in making verbal commitments about change by drawing parallels to how public commitment is asked for by witnesses in a trial (i.e., responding to the question "Do you swear to tell the truth…?" with "I do" rather than "I want to"). Similarly, in a traditional wedding ceremony, when both parties are asked to commit, they say, "I do" rather than "I hope so" or "I want to be able to."

Task 8. Switching Between MI and Other Methods. The final learning task for MI is knowing how and when to move flexibly among different methodologies, sometimes going beyond MI. MI appears to have better results with moving clients who are resistant to change on the path to committing to change; it appears to be less helpful with clients who are ready for immediate action.[14, 17] This is not to say that when applying other methods, agents are no longer collaborative, empathic, and respectful; rather, they continue within the spirit of MI as they deliver other interventions, such as *cognitive-behavioral* skill building or *social network enhancement.* Later, client ambivalence or resistance can signal the need to return to an MI style until the obstacle is resolved and the client can move forward again.

Miller and Rollnick[15] talk about different applications of MI as preludes to other services, as a style used throughout the treatment term as a fallback option returned to when clients exhibit resistance and/or ambivalence, and as an integrated component of a comprehensive set of services as outlined in the National Institute on Alcohol Abuse and Alcoholism's *Combined Behavioral Intervention Manual.*[18] MI is only one of several evidence-based practices for offender intervention that are supported by research. While MI is more likely to be most helpful for clients entering the change process, cognitive-behavioral skill building, social support enhancement (e.g., 12-step facilitation), and behavioral reinforcement applications *(contingency management)* may be equally or more important for some high-risk offenders to reclaim their lives from crime and deviance. The spirit of MI can continue through the use of these different modalities, but the actual skills that agents use may change. Knowing when to shift from one orientation and one tool to another is the mark of a skillful agent.

Learning MI is an ongoing process, and how far into the above stages any individual pursues proficiency is bound to be a personal choice as much as it is a function of his/her aptitude, commitment, and support. In the case of MI, the decision to build MI skills consistently is also likely to relate to values consistent with the essential ingredients of an MI style or orientation, which together encompass the MI spirit:

- Respect for an individual's autonomy and right to personal choice.

- Willingness to enter into collaborative partnerships with clients.

- The ability to see, expect, and draw out the best from clients.

Being able to identify an agent's MI learning stage can help give the agent more confidence and a practical focus to learning objectives. It will also make this guide more useful, not just in recognizing what stage of learning an agent is in, but also in supporting the learning of other stages.

Organizational Culture and How It Affects Learning MI

Thus far, this guide has provided an overview of the research on learning MI and the stages an agent goes through when acquiring proficiency in MI. However, in the field of corrections, people work within the boundaries of an agency with policies, attitudes, and a culture of its own. The agency or office culture a person works in can affect his/her attitude, opportunities, and rewards for learning MI. There are some fundamental differences in the barriers and supports for learning MI between an agent who works outside of an agency, more or less as an independent contractor, and an agent who works full time in a well-established organization. Compared to the individual working in an agency, the outside consultant is relatively unfettered by the organization's cultural notions about "the way we do business here." People working in almost any agency or office tend to share common ways of doing things over time, unspoken "know-how" and values[19] in which an outsider does not necessarily engage. These cultural aspects of an agency can either hinder or facilitate the learning of a new innovation like MI.

When the prevailing coworker mentality is one of skepticism and cynicism about changes to current practice, it may have a dampening effect on agents' learning in two fundamental ways. On one hand, there would likely be fewer people on staff who would model new preferred innovations and, on the other hand, practicing new skills in such an environment might invite critical judgments from colleagues. Therefore, not only is there limited support available for skill modeling, but there is also an atmosphere that hinders the practice of new skills.

The flipside to this scenario is also conceivable: an agency culture that provides norms that support and actively promote new and smart learning, i.e., *learning organizations.*[20–22] In learning organizations, positive recognition and rewards are available for staff actively learning new innovations.

Regardless of how their agencies are internally aligned, almost all corrections staff or agents must reckon with an organizational culture of some sort when learning MI, because corrections staff generally work within a "system" context. Corrections organizations can differ considerably in terms of the organizational culture but, generally, they share roots in a paramilitary orientation with varying degrees of allegiance to a command-and-control mental model.

Organizational hierarchy and structure is another manifestation of culture that may affect how MI is learned, primarily through the influence of first-line supervisors. Supervisors who are perceived as nonsupportive, indifferent, or cynical about the introduction of a new practice can cast a negative shadow on new innovations. This negativity can discourage even preliminary efforts to practice the new innovation despite the manifest policy of the organization. Moreover, supervision often works as a parallel process: the dynamics of the exchanges between staff superiors and subordinates (agents) is often acted out and reflected between the line staff and their clients.

Supervisors, therefore, play an important role in supporting the successful implementation of a new innovation. They can create a learning environment for subordinates that lowers the barriers to skill practice, observation, and feedback. They can also provide resources helpful for learning and supporting the formation of communities of practice, such as peer coaching groups.

There may be significant differences in access to resources helpful for learning (e.g., training and learning materials, schedule flexibility, formal feedback, and, most important, coaching and communities of practice). The ability to learn MI may be impeded or accelerated to the degree to which the availability of such resources varies, regardless of whether an individual works in or outside of an agency.

There are many reasons, therefore, to be mindful of the agency culture when introducing an important innovation such as MI. There are several areas where managers and supervisors can perform important roles in helping align the culture to support the implementation of MI. Such ideas of supervision, coaching, and supporting organizational culture shifts are further examined in chapter 4, "Assessing Motivational Interviewing Skills."

Endnotes

1. B.L. Burke, H. Arkowitz, and M. Menchola, "The Efficacy of Motivational Interviewing: A Meta-Analysis of Controlled Clinical Trials," *Journal of Counseling and Clinical Psychology* 71(5):843–61, 2003.

2. J. Hettema, J. Steele, and W.R. Miller, "Motivational Interviewing," *Annual Review of Clinical Psychology* 1(1):91–111, 2005.

3. S. Rubak, A. Sandbaek, T. Lauritzen, and B. Christensen, "Motivational Interviewing: A Systematic Review and Meta-Analysis," *British Journal of General Practice* 55(513):305–12, 2005.

4. E.I. Vasilaki, S.G. Hosier, and W.M. Cox, "The Efficacy of Motivational Interviewing as a Brief Intervention for Excessive Drinking: A Meta-Analytic Review," *Alcohol & Alcoholism* 41(3):328–35, 2006.

5. C. Trotter, *Working with Involuntary Clients: A Guide to Practice* (London, England: Sage, 1999).

6. C. Trotter, "The Supervision of Offenders— What Works?" in L. Noaks, M. Levi, and M. Maguire (eds.), *Contemporary Issues in Criminology* (Cardiff, UK: University of Wales Press, 1995), pp. 236–50.

7. W.R. Miller and K.A. Mount, "A Small Study of Training in Motivational Interviewing: Does One Workshop Change Clinician and Client

Behavior?" *Behavioural & Cognitive Psychotherapy* 29(4):457–71, 2001.

8. K.M. Carroll, S.A. Ball, C. Nich, S. Martino, T.L. Frankforter, C. Farentinos, L.E. Kunkel, S.K. Mikulich-Gilbertson, J. Morgenstern, J.L. Obert, D. Polcin, N. Snead, and G.E. Woody, "Motivational Interviewing to Improve Treatment Engagement and Outcome in Individuals Seeking Treatment for Substance Abuse: A Multisite Effectiveness Study," *Drug and Alcohol Dependence* 81(3):301–12, 2006.

9. S. Martino, S.A. Ball, S.L. Gallon, D. Hall, M. Garcia, S. Ceperich, S. Farentinos, J. Hamilton, and W. Hausotter, *Motivational Interviewing Assessment: Supervisory Tools for Enhancing Proficiency* (Salem, OR: Northwest Frontier Addiction Technology Transfer Center, Oregon Health and Science University, 2006).

10. W.R. Miller and T.B. Moyers, Eight stages in learning motivational interviewing. Unpublished research article, 2004.

11. W.R. Miller and T.B. Moyers, "Eight Stages in Learning Motivational Interviewing," *Journal of Teaching in the Addictions* 5(1):3–17, 2007.

12. W.R. Miller, C.E. Yahne, T.B. Moyers, J. Martinez, and M. Pirritano, "A Randomized Trial of Methods to Help Clinicians Learn Motivational Interviewing," *Journal of Consulting and Clinical Psychology* 72(6):1050–62, 2004.

13. C.E. Yahne, W.R. Miller, T.B. Moyers, and M. Pirritano, *Teaching Motivational Interviewing to Clinicians: A Randomized Trial of Training Methods* (Albuquerque, NM: Center on Alcoholism, Substance Abuse, and Addictions, 2004).

14. T.B. Moyers, T. Martin, P.J. Christopher, J.M. Houck, J.S. Tonigan, and P.C. Amrhein, "Client Language as a Mediator of Motivational Interviewing Efficacy: Where Is the Evidence?" *Alcoholism—Clinical and Experimental Research* 31(Suppl. 10):40S–47S, 2007.

15. W.R. Miller and S.R. Rollnick (eds.), *Motivational Interviewing: Preparing People for Change,* 2d ed. (New York: Guilford Press, 2002).

16. P.C. Amrhein, W.R. Miller, C.E. Yahne, M. Palmer, and L. Fulcher, "Client Commitment Language During Motivational Interviewing Predicts Drug Use Outcomes," *Journal of Consulting and Clinical Psychology* 71(5):862–78, 2003.

17. Project MATCH Research Group, "Project MATCH Secondary A Priori Hypotheses" *Addiction* 92(12):1671–98, 1997.

18. W.R. Miller (ed.), *Combined Behavioral Intervention Manual: A Clinical Research Guide for Therapists Treating People With Alcohol Abuse and Dependence.* COMBINE Monograph Series, vol. 1. (Bethesda, MD: U.S. Department of Health and Human Services, National Institute on Alcohol Abuse and Alcoholism, 2004.)

19. E.H. Schein, *Organizational Culture & Leadership* (San Francisco, CA: Jossey-Bass Publishers, 1989).

20. P.M. Senge, *The Fifth Discipline: The Art and Practice of Learning Organization,* 1st ed. (New York: Doubleday, 1990).

21. G. Suttler, *The Learning Organization* (New York: The Conference Board, 1995).

22. R.A. Rosenheck, "Organizational Process: A Missing Link Between Research and Practice," *Psychiatric Services* 52(12):1607–12, 2001.

CHAPTER 3 Supervising and Coaching To Support Implementation

Chapters 1 and 2 stressed that feedback and coaching were the most crucial factors to learning motivational interviewing (MI)[1] and, therefore, must be the focus of attention when considering a successful implementation of MI. This chapter wrestles with what successful implementation of MI means, who provides it, and what the differences are among supervising MI, coaching MI, clinical supervision, and quality assurance. This chapter also provides a framework for supervision and coaching, while chapter 4 addresses the actual methods used to assess skill and fidelity with MI. The ultimate goal is to implement MI in a manner that ensures that a good portion of the staff trained in MI is likely to become proficient enough in the method to effect changes in their clients.

Supervisors are the conduit for transferring ideas from administration and upper organizational management to line agents.[2] A supervisor's role can be an amalgam of the variety of hats—from championing innovation to providing quality assurance (QA)—that are needed for an implementation to be successful. However, it is important to be clear about what these different roles are and, more importantly, whether it should be the supervisor who always fills these roles. The four roles this chapter clarifies are supervising MI, providing clinical supervision, coaching MI, and providing quality assurance for MI.

Supervising MI

The role of a supervisor has an enormous effect on the successful implementation of a new innovation, whether or not the supervisor is skilled in the innovation.[3-9] Therefore, supervising the implementation of MI is about creating an atmosphere where MI can be learned, practiced, and coached successfully. It is more about creating conditions for skill acquisition and maintenance than about the nitty-gritty of reviewing skills and offering feedback and suggestions. There are several ways that supervisors can support the implementation of MI, whether or not they have skills or expertise in MI:

- **Creating cultural shifts.** The cultural and learning norms of the workplace affect staff's receptiveness to learning and implementing an innovation.[10-13] Supervisors have an understanding of these cultural norms and can therefore support a change in the culture. This has ramifications before and after training takes place. Often, agents know whether their supervisor thinks the training they are being sent to is important. Given this understanding of the culture and their ability to shape it, supervisors are able to enhance the anticipatory mindset of their staff before training, develop a foundation for subsequent practice of skills learned in the training, and remove barriers to receiving feedback about skills.[14]

- **Developing communities of practice.** After MI training, participants commonly express the need to practice their MI skills. This may require supervisors to develop a climate that facilitates and promotes cooperative study and practice. The supervisor can provide such an environment by supporting the formation of *peer coaching* groups, a forum for interest in MI (e.g., a *LISTSERV*), or communities of practice[15-18] that meet regularly to practice skills, role play difficult scenarios, and receive support and feedback.

A community of practice might initially consist of only two (or more) individuals in a local agency unit, e.g., the Pre-Sentencing Investigation Unit. As long as the agents agree to provide ongoing support to each other in their efforts to practice and acquire greater MI skills, the group constitutes a community of practice, no matter how informal. The more systematic the community becomes in its efforts to provide feedback and coaching around MI, the greater the probability that its members will grow in proficiency.

- **Mobilizing resources.** Supervisors have access to resources and are in the position to use existing resources efficiently. Resources in MI include reading material, taped demonstrations of skills, authorization of trainings, access to agents who are proficient in MI skills, and meeting space to practice skills. Mobilizing resources could be as basic as providing agents with helpful material on MI, but it could also include identifying champions of the innovation and relocating them to an area of greatest visibility so others can benefit from their skills. Supervisors can support ongoing MI coaching by identifying needed roles (such as peer coaches or quality assurance officers) and assigning them strategically. Finally, supervisors could promote and support outside coaching or clinical supervision for agents returning from an MI training workshop.

There are several other ways for supervisors to support the implementation of MI. Because supervisors are poised at such a key position in the organization, they can not only assess what the implementation needs are for their specific agency, but also follow through with the ideas they generate. Following is a summary of ways in which a supervisor can support the implementation of MI:

- Support the formation of peer coaching groups by providing a designated time—free of any administrative items—for peers to get together to focus on MI.

- Create an atmosphere that supports the giving and receiving of feedback.

- Participate in giving and receiving feedback, demonstrating a willingness to be vulnerable in the skill-acquisition process.

- Develop positive anticipation for MI training, for example, sending staff questions related to MI and providing incentives for the person with the most correct answers.

- Encourage staff to deepen their understanding of MI by rewarding them with further training or professional tape critiques.

- Make resources such as books and video demonstrations available to staff.

Thus far, the chapter has covered ideas for what supervisors can do without having expertise in MI. If they do have proficiency in MI, they can also support their staff's acquisition of MI skills by providing direct skill coaching, which mirrors clinical supervision.

Providing Clinical Supervision

Firstline supervisors have ongoing interactions with their staff related to providing general support to them, clarifying policies and procedures, conducting evaluations, and facilitating their overall professional growth. Clinical supervision is different from administrative supervision in that it is more focused on providing support and education, and facilitating growth of the agent's skills related to working with clients. In the health fields, particularly in addictions and mental health, practitioners (whether working at an agency or in private practice) receive ongoing clinical supervision. At a formal treatment agency, this clinical supervision may be provided by the practitioner's immediate supervisor or by the agency's designated clinical supervisor, who could also be someone who is not part of the agency but comes in solely to provide clinical supervision. In corrections, this job falls on the shoulders of firstline supervisors, whether or not they are trained in clinical supervision or are cognizant of the ramifications of providing it.

However, if supervisors indeed have the skills in MI to provide coaching, then their relationship with agents being coached begins to look like clinical supervision, which is further described in this chapter.

Falender and Shafranske[19] define clinical supervision as "education and training aimed at developing science-informed practice, facilitated through a collaborative interpersonal process [that] involves observation, evaluation, feedback, the facilitation of supervisee self-assessment, and the acquisition of knowledge and skills by instruction, modeling, and mutual problem solving." In clinical supervision and coaching, there is a *parallel process* in which the relationship or interaction between the supervisor and agent mirrors, informs, and shapes the relationship or interaction the agent develops with clients.

Clinical supervision usually focuses on helping agents develop:

- Self-awareness regarding how the agent is affecting and being affected by the client.

- Theory and knowledge, i.e., up-to-date information about the innovation.

- Skills in the agent's use of the innovation.

Purpose of Clinical Supervision

The purpose of clinical supervision as it relates to MI is to support agents in increasing their efficacy and expertise in using MI so as to be more effective with clients. More specifically, clinical supervision can be instrumental in helping agents to become more fluid in their abilities to shift strategies (e.g., directing, guiding, and following) within their dual system-defined roles.[20] Direct supervisors proficient in MI or designated clinical supervisors are therefore coaching the agent's skills in a systematic way.

The supervisory/coaching relationship requires much vulnerability on the part of the agent being coached. Being watched as one is struggling with skills and ways of managing a client can be threatening and awkward, especially if the person watching is someone who also completes annual evaluations that determine promotions and raises. Therefore, if clinical supervision or coaching is being provided by the agent's direct supervisor, a blurring of roles can occur. This needs to be clarified at the outset. Most importantly (and this is reemphasized in the section on coaching), there needs to be a clear understanding that the process of coaching an agent is *separate* from evaluating the agent.

Coaching MI

While the phenomenon of executive and personal coaching emerged only within the last 25 years, the concept of coaching another to improve skills is an ancient one that can be recognized in learning trades, parenting, teaching, or sports. It is founded on beliefs very similar to those of MI: that know-how needs to be drawn out of a person. In the case of coaching MI, the goal might be to increase MI-consistent behaviors and decrease MI-inconsistent behaviors through cooperative study, practice, and feedback. The prerequisites to being a coach include some level of proficiency with MI and a desire to support others in developing their MI skills. A coach could be a supervisor, a peer who agrees to coach another (perhaps reciprocally), a clinical supervisor, or an agent who is designated as an MI coach for his/her team.

Coaching is a flexible and versatile skill that can look very different based on the needs of the person being coached and the comfort of the coach. Focusing on the how, when, and what of coaching, Bacon and Spear[21] describe many ways that a coach could align with the person being coached. These approaches need to be looked at from the perspective of what the person being coached would like and what the coach is comfortable with.

Styles of Coaching

In looking at the "how" of coaching, Bacon and Spear describe the two poles as directive, where the person being coached is told what to do from the coach's perspective, and **nondirective,** where the relationship between the person being coached and the one doing the coaching is collaborative. The "when" of coaching is described as either when a need arises (i.e., circumstantial) or on a long-term, regular basis (i.e., programmatic). The "what" of coaching looks at whether the focus of coaching is to develop certain abilities and skills, which Bacon and Spear called specific, or to develop the whole person, which they called **holistic.** These concepts are illustrated in exhibit 3–1.

Now, applying these styles, one could say that coaching MI would generally be nondirective, programmatic, and specific. Bacon and Spear[21] call this overall style the "facilitator." Much like an MI practitioner, the facilitator coach has an interest in developing and supporting the skills of the person being coached by allowing that person to drive the coaching process, asking pertinent questions to help the person clarify gaps in skills, and offering suggestions for enhancing skills. However, when coaching MI, the style of coaching will change based on the needs of the agent being coached. For example, if an agent asks for a more directive approach to coaching only when the need arises, this style would be called the "manager," whose focus would be on short-term, specific improvements in skills.

Thus, there are four main points concerning coaching styles or types:

1. Coaching is universal.

2. Coaching is a role that can be performed by:

   - Trainers.
   - Firstline supervisors.
   - Clinical supervisors.
   - Peers.
   - Designated coaches.

3. The styles (approach and scope) of coaching vary along three continua (how, when, and what) according to whatever two individuals negotiate as important.

4. In common practice, coaching for MI (and possibly other evidence-based practices) is likely to be limited to a few styles like facilitator and manager.

Ideas for Peer Coaching

The following are some suggestions about the structure and focus of coaching sessions adapted from the work of William Miller, Kathy Jackson, and Mary O'Leary:[22]

- Set regular meetings where the explicit focus is on developing MI skills.

- Role play difficult situations with clients to gather different ways of using MI skills to handle such situations.

EXHIBIT 3–1: INGREDIENTS IN THE STYLES OF COACHING

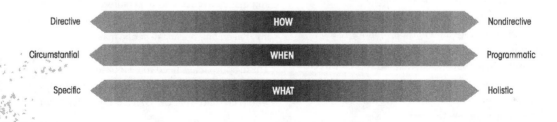

Directive	HOW	Nondirective
Circumstantial	WHEN	Programmatic
Specific	WHAT	Holistic

- Discuss readings, taped "expert" demonstrations, or theoretical issues to deepen understanding of MI.

- Take turns taping sessions and use meetings to review and discuss tapes. (See chapter 4 for instructions on using coding tools to analyze taped content.)

- Decide on personal challenges that you are willing to focus on between meetings, for example, focusing on complex versus simple reflections.

Steps to Coaching

Australian researcher Chris Trotter[23–25] investigated probation officers and neglect case social workers for more than 20 years to find out what was different about those who had better outcomes with involuntary clients. The four skills he identified were (1) clarifying roles, (2) developing a working alliance, (3) mutual problem solving, and (4) modeling skills. As mentioned earlier, there is a parallel between how a coach works with an agent and how the agent in turn works with a client. Therefore, the skills that Trotter outlines in working with clients parallel the steps used to structure coaching sessions.

1. **Role clarification and agreements.** The process of coaching begins with being clear about the parameters. Specifically, these include agreements on the kind of coaching relationship (mutual between peers or one way), when and how frequently coaching sessions will take place, and what the coaching session will look like (e.g., reviewing a taped contact, sitting in a live contact, demonstrating an MI-adherent contact, or role-playing using MI in difficult situations). This agenda-setting process,[26] which is so crucial when working with clients, is also important when coaching. The collective agreement is a commitment to practice MI and support each other or the person being coached in deepening MI skills.

2. **Working alliance.** Creating an effective, trusting coaching relationship is the cornerstone of successful coaching. Coaching relationships that embody the MI spirit are collaborative, respectful of the autonomy of the person being coached, and evocative, i.e., bringing out problems and their solutions from the person being coached. If a supervisor is doing the coaching, the distinction between coaching and administrative supervision (evaluation) needs to be clear.

3. **Assessment.** Just as it is important to assess what stage of change a client is in, it is also important to discuss what stage of learning[27] the agent being coached is in. (See chapter 2, "How Motivational Interviewing Is Learned," for an overview of the tasks for learning MI.) There are several microcomponents in MI to be assessed. (See book II, *Exercises for Developing MI Skills in Corrections,* for information on the components of MI.) Apart from the focused assessment of skills, it is important to evoke from the agent what his/her struggles with MI are and what he/she would like to have as the focus of the coaching session. In this way, the coach is at the service of the agent, offering suggestions and asking questions when needed but mostly listening to the agent being coached.

4. **Feedback.** While feedback may include providing agents with information on their skills, sharing spirit, and managing the change process (as discussed in *Exercises for Developing MI Skills in Corrections*), feedback can also include modeling MI-adherent skills for the agent, not only in the coaching relationship but also in live contacts with clients.

Thus, the results of a successful coaching relationship extend beyond enhancing the MI skills of the agent being coached. Collaborative relationships between peers help solve implementation problems and can act to model parallel processes between agents and clients. The relationship that develops between the coach and the agent becomes one of trust, vulnerability, and willingness to learn through support. The effects of this relationship can therefore transfer to the relationship that agents have with their clients.

Providing Quality Assurance

Quality assurance (QA) is the process of evaluating a particular practice, in this case the use of MI, to see if it is meeting standards set for the particular practice. While the focus of coaching and supervision is on supporting and enhancing the agent's skills, the immediate focus of QA is a quantitative one that looks at how the agent rates with regard

Conclusion

This chapter discusses the four categories of roles a supervisor may play in ensuring the successful implementation of MI. The four categories include administrative supervision, clinical supervision, coaching, and quality assurance. While there is considerable overlap among these roles as they relate to MI, this chapter focused on parsing out and clarifying the significant differences, as illustrated in exhibit 3–3.

EXHIBIT 3–2: TOOLS AVAILABLE TO ASSESS COMPONENTS OF MOTIVATIONAL INTERVIEWING

| TOOL | CRITERIA | | | | |
	Interviewer Skills	Client Responses	Spirit Adherence	Timing of Interactions	Management of Change Process
BECCI	Likert Scale		Likert Scale	Likert Scale	Likert Scale
MISC	Actual Counts	Actual Counts	Likert Scale	Actual Counts	
MITI	Actual Counts	Actual Counts	Likert Scale	Actual Counts	
V-MIC	Actual Counts	Actual Counts	Likert Scale	Actual Counts	
YACS	Likert Scale		Likert Scale		Likert Scale

BECCI = Behavior Change Counseling Index, MISC = Motivational Interviewing Skill Code, MITI = Motivational Interviewing Treatment Integrity, V-MIC = Versatile Motivational Interview Critique, YACS = Yale Adherence and Competence Scale

to certain criteria. QA lends itself to the use of tools and can be done by anyone who can recognize the elements that are being looked for in the tool, with or without the actual ability to demonstrate the skills themselves. QA can also be combined with any of the roles discussed in this chapter.

There are several tools that use different methods to measure a variety of QA criteria. While the next chapter discusses these tools, methods, and criteria indepth, exhibit 3–2 provides a summary of the tools currently available to assess the different components of MI.

The focus of administrative supervision is to support the implementation of MI. These kinds of support aim to create the most conducive atmosphere for learning MI. The style of supervision can be impersonal.

Clinical supervision of MI focuses on both the content and the process of learning and using MI. It is not only concerned with proficiency in MI but also the overall development of the agent as a corrections practitioner. The relationship style is extremely personal in nature, focusing acutely on the individual being supervised. There is a hierarchy inherent in the relationship in terms of knowledge, and the relationship tends to be long term.

EXHIBIT 3-3: FOUR ROLES OF A SUPERVISOR IN SUPPORTING SUCCESSFUL MI IMPLEMENTATION

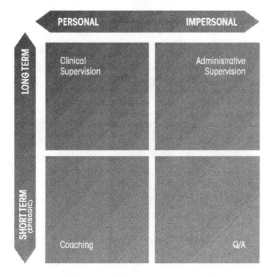

Coaching focuses on enhancing proficiency in MI and can be done by supervisors, peers, or a designated coach. There is not an inherent hierarchy in the relationship, and while it is personal, the relationship tends to be more short term.

Finally, quality assurance focuses on reviewing practice and comparing it with criteria. It is an impersonal process with no hierarchical components in the relationship, and the relationship tends to be short term.

Endnotes

1. W.R. Miller, C.E. Yahne, T.B. Moyers, J. Martinez, and M. Pirritano, "A Randomized Trial of Methods To Help Clinicians Learn Motivational Interviewing," *Journal of Consulting and Clinical Psychology* 72(6):1050–62, 2004.

2. H. Risher, "Fostering a Performance-Driven Culture in the Public Sector," *Public Manager* 36(3):51–56, 2007.

3. D. Fixsen, S.F. Naoom, K.A. Blase, R.M. Friedman, and F. Wallace, *Implementation Research: A Synthesis of the Literature* (Tampa, FL: University of South Florida, Louis de la Parte Florida Mental Health Institute, The National Implementation Research Network, 2005).

4. T.E. Backer, R.P. Liberman, and T.G. Kuehnel, "Dissemination and Adoption of Innovative Psychosocial Interventions," *Journal of Consulting and Clinical Psychology* 54(1):111–18, 1986.

5. K.J. Klein and J.S. Sorra, "The Challenge of Innovation Implementation." *Academy of Management Review* 21(4):1055–80, 1996.

6. D.D. Simpson, "A Conceptual Framework for Transferring Research to Practice," *Journal of Substance Abuse Treatment* 22(4):171–82, 2002.

7. P. Gendreau and C. Goggin, "The Forgotten Issue in Effective Correctional Treatment: Program Implementation," *International Journal of Offender Therapy & Comparative Criminology* 43(2):180, 1999.

8. W.R. Miller, T.B. Moyers, L. Arciniega, D. Ernst, and A. Forcehimes, "Training, Supervision and Quality Monitoring of the COMBINE Study Behavioral Interventions," *Journal of Studies on Alcohol* 66(4):188–95, 2005.

9. S. Fernandez and D.W. Pitts, "Under What Conditions Do Public Managers Favor and Pursue Organizational Change?" *The American Review of Public Administration* 37(3):324–41, 2007.

10. R.H. Moos, "Addictive Disorders in Context: Principles and Puzzles of Effective Treatment and Recovery," *Psychology of Addictive Behaviors* 17(1):3–12, 2003.

11. R.H. Moos and B.S. Moos, "The Staff Workplace and the Quality and Outcome of Substance Abuse Treatment," *Journal Studies of Alcohol* 59(1):43–51, 1998.

12. P.W. Corrigan, L. Steiner, S.G. McCracken, B. Blaser, and M. Barr, "Strategies for Disseminating Evidence-Based Practices to Staff Who Treat People With Serious Mental Illness," *Psychiatric Services* 52(12):1598–1606, 2001.

13. G.A. Aarons and A.C. Sawitzky, "Organizational Culture and Climate and Mental Health Provider Attitudes Toward Evidence-Based Practice," *Psychological Services* 3(1):61–72, 2006.

14. "Implementing Motivational Interviewing in Correctional Settings: An Interview with Dr. Miller," 2009.

15. C.D. Norman and T. Huerta, "Knowledge Transfer & Exchange Through Social Networks: Building Foundations for a Community of Practice Within Tobacco Control," *Implementation Science* 1(September):20, 2006.

16. R.A. Rosenheck, "Organizational Process: A Missing Link Between Research and Practice." *Psychiatric Services* 52(12):1607–12, 2001.

17. E.L. Lesser and J. Storck, "Communities of Practice and Organizational Performance," *IBM Systems Journal* 40(4):6, 2001.

18. E. Sauve, "Informal Knowledge Transfer," *Training + Development* 61(3):22–24, 2007.

19. C.A. Falender and E.P. Shafranske, *The Practice of Clinical Supervision: A Competency-Based Approach* (Washington, DC: American Psychological Association, 2004).

20. J.L. Skeem, L.E. Louden, D. Polaschek, and J. Camp, "Assessing Relationship Quality in Mandated Community Treatment: Blending Care With Control," *Psychological Assessment* 19(4):397–410, 2007.

21. T.R. Bacon and K.I. Spear, *Adaptive Coaching: The Art and Practice of a Client-Centered Approach to Performance Improvement* (Mountain View, CA: Davies-Black Publishing, 2003).

22. W.R. Miller, K. Jackson, and M. O'Leary, *Suggestions on Structure and Focus of Coaching Sessions* (Boulder, CO: Justice System Analysis and Training, 2008).

23. C. Trotter, *Working with Involuntary Clients* (London: Sage, 1999).

24. C. Trotter, "The Impact of Different Supervision Practices in Community Corrections: Cause for Optimism," *Australian and New Zealand Journal of Criminology* 29(1):29–46, 1996.

25. C. Trotter, "The Supervision of Offenders: What Works?" in L. Noaka, M. Levi, and M. Maguire (eds.), *Contemporary Issues in Criminology* (Cardiff, UK: University of Wales Press, 1995).

26. S. Rollnick, W.R. Miller, and C.C. Butler, *Motivational Interviewing in Health Care: Helping Patients Change Behavior* (New York: Guilford Press, 2008).

27. W.R. Miller and T.B. Moyers, "Eight Stages in Learning Motivational Interviewing," *Journal of Teaching in the Addictions* 5(1):15, 2006.

CHAPTER 4

Assessing Motivational Interviewing Skills

Chapter 3 defined the interpersonal approaches that supervisors or teams may use to help agents develop proficiency in motivational interviewing (MI) skills. This chapter discusses the quality assurance (QA) MI skill rating systems that supervisors or teams may use to enhance these approaches. Quality assurance rating systems assess agents' levels of skill in the use of MI and provide them with written or numeric feedback about areas of skill proficiency and/or need for improvement. Subsequent periodic ratings show agents how they have improved with practice, additional training, and/or coaching.

Coaching Based on Feedback From Skills Assessments

Once staff have been trained in MI, the next step to successful on-the-job implementation is assessment of the extent to which they are able to apply MI skills in the workplace. Periodically measuring staff's use of MI skills, not just their understanding of the theories of MI, in particular work contexts is essential for a variety of reasons.

First, the research on implementation and training in human services and research specific to MI training over the past decade indicate that skills learned in training will not transfer to on-the-job use unless they are followed up with performance measurements, skill-based coaching, and organizational support.[1–3] Skill assessment identifies the skills that agents must practice during coaching sessions. Skill assessment also measures improvements or declines in staff MI skill use over time, the results of which are foundational to MI quality

assurance procedures. After fulfilling posttraining coaching procedures, ongoing skill measurements can become the basis for clinical supervision discussions that help with long-term skill acquisition and competency development.

In addition to assisting MI-specific implementation, periodic skill assessment supports the implementation of evidence-based practices (EBP). "Measuring relevant processes and practices" and "providing measurement feedback" are the final two of the eight evidence-based principles for effective interventions recommended by the National Institute of Corrections manual on implementing evidence-based practices in community corrections.[4] EBP implementation requires regular measurement of processes and procedures in order to provide policymakers, managers, and line staff with the feedback they need to correct the natural tendency to "drift" away from careful fidelity and return to the models of EBP theories and programs. Without measurement and feedback, programs that are ostensibly evidence based can vary so significantly from the original EBP models over time that the outcome improvements expected from implementation of EBP diminish or disappear. Measuring MI skills and providing feedback helps agencies become accustomed to the kinds of regular normative performance measurements that are necessary to sustain a variety of EBP.

The MI skill assessment process requires staff to understand and dialogue about the skills they are using and the more subtle dynamics of agent-client interactions that often go unnoticed. Coaching sessions that focus on specific skill improvement goals allow staff to practice more closely, attending to client reactions and stances toward behavior change. When coaches and staff have the opportunity to work together to break down longer interactions into specific components, staff can learn new ways of hearing their clients. This heightened awareness facilitates the task 3 MI learning goals of identifying and reinforcing client change talk. As staff become more aware of the specific things they do that contribute to enhancing clients' intrinsic motivation to change, staff are better able to replicate these change-inviting interactions. Growing awareness of client statements about change helps staff avoid missing opportunities to reinforce these prosocial statements and lead clients further down the change path.

Skills Assessed in MI Evaluation

Any reliable method of MI assessment will aim to measure the extent to which a staff-client interaction embodies the basic components of MI. Because MI is a method of interacting with people, there are three potential elements of an interaction to assess: (1) how the agent contributes to the interaction, (2) how the client contributes, and (3) how the two of them are working together. See exhibit 4–1 for a visual representation of these elements.

These three elements may each be assessed by how well they conform to the standard MI principles: express empathy, develop discrepancy, roll with resistance, and support self-efficacy.[5] Regarding self-efficacy, an evaluator might ask:

1. How well did the agent appear to support the client's self-efficacy?

2. What evidence did the client give of feeling supported?

3. How well did the staff and client seem to work together with regard to this support?

To be truly comprehensive, an assessment of an agent's interaction would need to consider adherence to the MI principles and the use of recommended types of interactions between the agent and the client. Because this level of complexity presents quite a challenge for assessment, over the past 20 years researchers have created a variety of assessment tools and methods that hone in on particular aspects of MI within specific settings.

History of MI Skill Assessment

Initially, MI trainers tried to measure on-the-job implementation of MI skills with paper-and-pencil questionnaires like the Helpful Responses Questionnaire (HRQ)[6] or the HRQ for criminal justice settings by Scott Walters. The HRQ requires trainees to respond to six hypothetical client statements with "what they would say next." Trainee responses are then assigned numeric values according to their adherence to MI principles and summed for a total score. While such questionnaires may be helpful for measuring increases in *knowledge about* MI before and after training, they are poor predictors of trainees' abilities to *implement* MI skills on the job.[7]

EXHIBIT 4–1: THREE ELEMENTS OF INTERACTIONS USED TO ASSESS ADHERENCE TO MI PRINCIPLES

Rosengren and colleagues hypothesized that one reason for the poor correlations between paper-and-pencil questionnaires and MI skill implementation might be the noninteractive written material presented to trainees. They responded by creating the Video Assessment of Simulated Encounters (VASE-R).[8] For the VASE-R, trainees provide 18 written responses to 3 video vignettes of agents doing MI. Responses are rated on a 0–2 scale according to their adherence to MI principles, and then combined to form five subscale scores and one total score. Despite its more interactive format, however, the VASE-R still measures posttraining written responses, rather than on-the-job skill implementation.

Evaluating how well trainees use MI skills with clients in the workplace requires observation and measurement of agent-client interactions. This can be done by placing an observer in the session room, or by audio- or videotaping sessions. Either method has the potential to change interactions between agents and clients, as people tend to behave differently when they know they are being observed. Because many people find it easier to tune out once their session is underway, and because session tapes allow evaluators to stop and start the tape rather than being confined to real time, most evaluation systems recommend audio or video recording rather than direct observation.

Currently, there are several approaches to evaluating interactions between MI agents and clients. These approaches vary in length and difficulty of training time, ease of use, the kinds of MI skills they consider, ease of sustaining inter-rater reliability, the settings for which they were designed, and the degree to which they assess client responses. Though interview evaluation methods vary, certain terms referring to elements of MI tend to appear in multiple skill measurement approaches. Understanding these terms is the first step in deciding which elements of MI are key for staff performance measurement in a given agency setting.

Common MI Interview Tape Assessment Terms

The following terms in bold refer to common terms that several types of rating systems use to describe the general sets of agent-client dynamics that are evaluated during taped interviews:

- **Tape evaluators.** These individuals review entire interviews or specified tape segments and evaluate their content according to definitions assigned to global measures.

- **Global measures.** Reference points against which agent-client behaviors can be evaluated. "Global" refers to the fact that the entire interview is being evaluated as a whole, rather than parsed into individual interactions that are evaluated separately. The "measures" vary according to the rating system, but may include those listed in exhibit 4–2.

- **Global impressions.** An evaluator's overall impression of the interpersonal interactions during an entire taped segment or during a specified interview segment. These impressions are assigned a numeric value on a Likert scale (e.g., 1 = low to 7 = high) to facilitate comparison with later interview submissions or group averages.

- **Agent behavior counts.** Because global impressions are subject to evaluator bias, and because some evaluations capture broader, overall impressions of the use of MI-related strategies, it is helpful for evaluators to assign categories to individual agent utterances. Evaluators then calculate the percentages of utterances by category and compare them to ideal skill use percentages—those skill percentages that correspond to decreases in client defensiveness and/or increases in positive client outcomes according to research. Where research has yet to be completed, these ideal percentages may be based on expert opinion. These agent behavior counts help supervisors identify agent strengths that should be commended and reinforced, as well as areas that should be practiced or made into long-term skill acquisition goals.

EXHIBIT 4-2: GLOBAL MEASURES

Acceptance	Affect	Benefit (from the session)
Acknowledging challenges	Cooperation	Collaboration
Affirming strengths	Disclosure	
Change planning	Engagement	
Collaboration	Resistance	
Direction	Self-exploration	
Egalitarianism		
Elicitation of motivation to change		
Empathy (expressing understanding)		
Evocation		
Exploring ambivalence		
Genuineness		
Heightening discrepancies		
MI spirit/style		
Summarizing		
Supporting client autonomy/self-efficacy		
Warmth		

Exhibit 4–3 shows a partial list of agent behavior counts that appear in a variety of coding systems and a classification of these behavior types, respectively.

- **Adherence.** The way that some agents use MI skills, whether they follow the principles and theories precisely or only to a degree. Exhibit 4–3 includes a list of adherent behavior types.

- **Client behavior counts.** The measurable effects of agents' use of MI skills on clients. In the past 10 years, clinical trials have shown significant links between client statements of commitment to change in MI interviews and actual improvements in target behavior outcomes.[9, 10] Agencies that want to determine whether agent MI skill use is leading clients to make the kinds of statements that correspond to behavior change use coding systems that track client responses. Exhibit 4–4 shows a list of client behavior counts.

Common MI Interview Tape Evaluation Systems

Having listed the common terms and rating measures for a variety of approaches to evaluating agent-client interactions, this chapter now

EXHIBIT 4-3: AGENT BEHAVIOR COUNTS

MI-Adherent Agent Behaviors	MI Nonadherent Agent Behaviors	Neutral
Affirming	Advising	Facilitating
Asking open questions	Asking closed questions	Offering personal feedback
Emphasizing client control	Confronting	Providing filler
Giving information after asking the client for permission	Directing	Providing structure
Paraphrasing	Giving information without asking the client for permission	Raising concern
Providing a complex reflection	Warning	Self-disclosing
Providing a simple reflection		
Reframing		
Rephrasing		
Summarizing		
Supporting		

summarizes the various rating systems that are most commonly used in criminal justice settings or ones that might easily be adapted for use. Exhibit 4–5 provides an easy reference comparison of the processes, strengths, and weaknesses of each tool. Exhibit 4–6 indicates which global measures and behavior counts are included in each rating system. Several rating systems are described here.

Behavior Change Counseling Index—Criminal Justice Version (BECCI-CJ). This tool was initially designed to measure posttraining gains in the use of behavior change counseling skills. Behavior change counseling is an adaptation of MI often used in healthcare settings. Raters read the BECCI-CJ manual and watch a training video before listening to in-person or recorded sessions. They score 11 items on a 0–4 scale, then calculate an average of the ratings that can be used to provide

feedback to the agent about additional training or practice needs. The tool is easy to learn and use, and it has shown moderate to good inter-rater reliability in clinical trials with simulated consultations.[11] The criminal justice system version of the tool and manual can be downloaded from the Web at *www.motivationalinterview.org/library.*

SCENARIO: ADHERENCE

Adherence Using Affirmations

The MISC 2.0 rating system defines affirmations as agent statements that convey something positive or complimentary to the client, whether that is appreciation for a client's efforts, confidence in the client's abilities, or "applause" for something the client did well. This is an important skill for helping clients feel supported so that they are willing to consider change, but using too many affirmations may make the client feel that the agent is not being genuine. So overuse of this skill would not be consistent with MI theory, despite the fact that the skill itself is classified as MI adherent.

Adherence Using Closed Questions

In another example, the MISC 2.0 defines closed questions as those that require a one-word answer: yes, no, a specific fact, or a certain number. If kept to a minimum, using closed questions may be MI adherent. But many agents tend to overuse closed questions and make obtaining concrete details the focus of the session, rather than gaining understanding of the client's perspective through open questions that explore ambivalence about change. It is only this overuse that is MI nonadherent.

EXHIBIT 4-4: CLIENT BEHAVIOR COUNTS

Change Talk	Sustain Talk	Resistance	Neutral
Expressing a desire to change	Expressing a desire not to change	Arguing	Asking a question
Expressing a need to change	Expressing a need not to change	Interrupting	Following
Expressing ability to/optimism for change	Expressing commitment not to change	Negating	
Expressing commitment to change	Expressing inability to change	Not following	
Expressing concern about the status quo	Other indications of movement away from change		
Other indications of movement toward change	Providing reasons not to change		
Providing reasons to change	Reporting steps taken away from change		
Recognizing a problem			
Reporting steps taken toward change			

Motivational Interviewing Skill Code (MISC 1.0 and 2.0). The MISC 1.0 tool requires three reviews of an interview tape or segment to allow for an evaluator's indepth evaluation of the interactions between agent dynamics (27 behavior categories, 6 global measures), client responses (4 behavior categories, 4 global measures), and the relationship between agent and client (2 global measures). Its breadth and detail made it the gold standard for evaluating the use of MI for research and publications. After several validation and outcome studies, the tool was revised into the MISC 2.0, which requires only two reviews of each tape. The MISC 2.0 includes 19 agent behavior categories and 3 agent global measures. Only 1 client global measure is included and client behaviors are classified into 6 categories of change or sustain talk, rated on a –5 to +5 scale. The complexity of this coding system poses difficulties for inter-rater reliability, which was moderate overall in validation studies.[12-15] After raters first learn MISC 2.0, they typically require 40 hours of training over a 3-month period, followed by weekly review sessions to

SCENARIO: CATEGORIZING CLIENT RESPONSES

Consider a scenario in which the desired client behavior change was having the client attend a 12-step program to eliminate drug use. The agent asks, "What are your thoughts about attending a program like Narcotics Anonymous to get support for your goal of staying clean?"

Client response #1: *I'd really like to try that.*

This client response is an example of change talk, indicating a desire to move in that direction.

Client response #2: *I've been trying that and last week I decided I'm not going back there.*

This client response is an example of sustain talk, reporting steps taken away from that particular change direction.

Client response #3: *That's a stupid idea. Don't tell me how I need to get clean.*

This client response is an example of resistance, arguing against the suggestion and the agent.

Client response #4: *You think I should consider that?*

This client response is neutral because the client simply responds with a question that follows the agent's question.

sustain inter-rater reliability. For this reason, the tool may be best suited to indepth process research rather than training and practice applications. MISC 1.0 and 2.0 manuals may be downloaded at *http://casaa.unm.edu/ codinginst.html.*

Client Language Assessment of Motivational Interviewing (CLAMI or MISC 2.1). This tool revises the client behavior ratings of the MISC 2.0 and provides a supplement to be used with other coding systems that rate only agent behaviors and global measures. The CLAMI classifies client utterances into eight categories and rates the global measure of client resistance on a Likert scale. Raters create transcripts of the entire session and then code client utterances from the transcript while listening to the interview. Training time is not yet determined, though any time would be in addition to training time for the accompanying rating systems that evaluate only agent behaviors. The 2006 draft of the CLAMI may be downloaded at *http://casaa.unm.edu/codinginst.html.*

Motivational Interviewing Treatment Integrity (MITI 2.0 and 3.0). Whereas the MISC was designed to answer the process questions of how various agent MI skill levels interact with client responses, the MITI focuses on the simpler questions of how closely agent behaviors resemble MI and where skills might be improved. The MITI 2.0 classifies agent behaviors into seven categories and rates two agent global measures on a 1–7 scale. Lack of clarity on global rankings led to the MITI 3.0 revision, which includes five global measure rankings on a 1–5 scale with differential criteria for each ranking. The MITI does not

---

AGENT BEHAVIOR TYPES

- **MI Adherent**—Ways of interacting with clients that are consistent with MI principles and theories.

- **MI Nonadherent**—Ways of interacting with clients that are inconsistent with MI principles and theories.

- **Neutral**—Skills that neither support nor go against MI principles and theories.

BROAD CATEGORIES OF CLIENT BEHAVIOR COUNTS

- **Change talk**—Client statements indicating preparation for, commitment to, or steps taken toward positive behavior changes.

- **Sustain talk**—Client statements favoring continuation of the status quo, rather than moving toward change.

- **Resistance**—Client statements that indicate dissonance in the agent-client relationship, where the resistance is against the agent, not against making a change.

- **Neutral**—Client statements that neither move toward nor away from change or indicate tension with the agent.

---

assess client behaviors or global measures. Agent feedback includes global measure rankings and four agent skill use percentages that may be compared to beginning proficiency and competency standards established by expert opinion. MITI coder training involves manual reading and 30–40 hours of training, followed by periodic review sessions. With fewer coding classifications than the MISC, the MITI demonstrated good to excellent inter-rater reliability in validation studies.[14] The MITI 2.0 and 3.0 manuals may be downloaded at *http://casaa.unm.edu/codinginst.html.*

Versatile Motivational Interview Critique (V-MIC). This evaluation system combines the behavior categories and global measures of the MITI 3.0 with the client change talk types and strength ratings of the MISC 2.0 to allow for optimum inter-rater reliability, while also tracking client responses that are predictive of behavior change. Raters listen once or twice to taped interviews, and

EXHIBIT 4-5: COMPARISON OF MI SKILL USE EVALUATION SYSTEMS

	BECCI-CJ (2003)	MISC 1.0 (2000)	MISC 2.0 (2003)	MISC 2.1/CLAMI (2006)
What is Rated	**Interview Tapes**	**Session Tapes**	**Session Tapes**	**Session Transcripts in Addition to Tapes**
Focus	Assess improvements in behavior change counseling (an adaptation of MI), focusing on understanding the client (not change talk elicitation).	Indepth evaluation of the relationship between agent behaviors and client change talk.	Indepth evaluation of the relationship between agent behaviors and client change talk.	Assess client language and behaviors, providing a supplement to other coding systems that only consider agent behaviors.
Evaluation Process	Complete an 11-item questionnaire, rating items on a 0–4 scale.	Listen to 20-minute tape segments three times; rate 6 therapist, 4 client, and 2 relationship global measures on a 1–7 scale; classify every agent utterance into 27 categories and every client utterance into 4 categories.	Listen to full sessions twice; rate 1 client and 3 agent global measures on a 1–7 scale; classify every agent utterance into 19 categories; classify client utterances into 6 change talk categories.	Listen to the full session once while reading the session transcript; classify client utterances into 8 categories; rate client resistance on a Likert scale.
Resulting Feedback	Average numeric score; 1–3 rank on how much the interviewer talked.	Client and agent global measures rankings; skill use percentages compared to expert and threshold proficiency standards; agent talk time percentages; client response type percentages.	Client and agent global measures rankings; agent skill use totals or frequency counts compared to expert and threshold proficiency standards; client change talk types and totals.	Client behavior category totals and Likert scale global measure rankings.
Validation, Reliability, and Outcome Studies	Construct and internal validity of tool items and inter-rater reliability (Lane et al. 2005).	Content validity (de Jonge et. al. 2005); reliability (Moyers et al. 2003, de Jonge et al. 2005, Tappin et al. 2000); construct validity (Miller and Mount 2001).	Outcomes (Amrhein et al. 2003).	MISC 2.0 studies.
Evaluator Training	Background reading, manual reading, training video.	Manual reading; 40 hours of training (over 3 months) or until >80% inter-rater reliability is attained; periodic (weekly) review sessions.	Manual reading; 40 hours of training (over 3 months) or until >80% inter-rater reliability is attained; periodic (weekly) review sessions.	Not yet specified.
Strengths	Minimal training required; tool quickly identifies skills that need more training; can be used repeatedly for gain scores; moderate to good inter-rater reliability.	Good for indepth process research on MI and linking agent behaviors to client responses.	Good for indepth process research on MI and linking agent behaviors to client responses.	Can be used to supplement other rating tools that do not consider client behaviors.
Weaknesses	Measures BCC, not MI; tested on simulated consultations only; does not address client behaviors; no competency standards provided.	Intensive 3-month training; difficult to maintain inter-rater reliability with so many coding classifications; labor intensive; shares moderate reliability in research.	Intensive 3-month training; difficult to maintain inter-rater reliability with so many coding classifications; labor intensive; shares moderate reliability of MISC 1.0.	Transcripts are time consuming to create; is not a stand-alone time tool for agent assessment so it would require additional rating training.

MITI 2.0 (2003)	MITI 3.0 (2007)	VASE-R (2005)	V-MIC (2007)	YACS II (2005)
		Trainee Written Responses to 3 Acted Video Vignettes		
Session Tapes	**Session Tapes**		**Session Tapes**	**Session Tapes**
Measuring MI use for clinical trials; providing feedback for improving agent adherence to MI; measuring training effectiveness.	Measuring MI use for clinical trials; providing feedback for improving agent adherence to MI; measuring training effectiveness.	Providing efficient, cost-effective, interaction-based, one-time assessment of MI skill in written responses.	Providing agents with feedback and/or coaching on MI strength and growth areas; allowing agency, national database, and gain score comparisons; tracking correlations between agent skills and client change talk.	Measuring agent adherence and competence in delivering general and specific treatment modalities, including MI for research.
Listen to 20-minute session segments once; rate 2 agent global measures on a 1–7 scale; classify agent utterances into 7 categories.	Listen to 20-minute session segments once; rate 5 agent global measures on a 1–5 scale; classify agent utterances into 7 categories.	Rate 18 trainee written responses to 3 video vignettes on a 0–2 scale.	Listen once to full 20- to 60-minute sessions; use the MITI 3.0 coding system to report global measures and behavior count percentages; use MISC 2.0 ratings of the type and strength of client change talk; generate software graphs and written feedback for agents to use in followup coaching.	Listen once to full session; take notes and tally interactions in up to 69 item categories; rate items on 1–7 scales for frequency/extensiveness and skill level/competence.
Agent global measure rankings; 4 agent skill use percentages/ratios compared to beginning proficiency and competency standards.	Agent global measure rankings; 4 agent skill use percentages/ratios compared to beginning proficiency and competency standards.	Five subscale scores and a total score, compared to suggested proficiency values.	Software-generated report including: graphed agent, agency, and national database skill percentage averages and summary "skill balance" scores; agent global measure rankings; client change talk per hour totals; individualized written feedback on agent strength and growth areas.	Likert scale rankings on skill use frequency and level for 9 MI items and up to 60 additional items.
Factor analysis on the MISC, inter-rater reliability, sensitivity (Moyers et al. 2005).	MITI 2.0 studies.	Internal reliability and concurrent validity (Rosengren et al. 2005).	MITI 2.0 studies; MISC 2.0 studies; correlations between agent behaviors and change talk available from J-SAT.	No validations for YACS II MI items; YACS I reliability, factor structure, concurrent, and discriminant validity (Carroll et al. 2000, Madson et al. 2005).
Manual reading; 40 hours of training or until >80% inter-rater reliability is attained; periodic (weekly) review sessions.	Manual reading; 40 hours of training or until >80% inter-rater reliability is attained; periodic (weekly) review sessions.	Background reading; manual reading; 4–8 hours of training for inter-rater reliability.	Manual reading; 30–40 hours of training or until >80% inter-rater reliability is attained; periodic (weekly) review sessions.	Manual reading; 30–40 hours of training and 10 practice inter-rater tapes; periodic review sessions.
Quicker and easier to code than the MISC; good to excellent inter-rater reliability.	Quicker and easier to code than the MISC; includes clearer descriptions for global measures than the MISC or the MITI 2.0.	Video formats are more engaging than paper questionnaires; brief 35-minute testing time; shorter coder training; adequate inter-rater reliability.	Provides comparisons to agency and 5-year database averages; reports client change talk averages; provides individualized skill improvement suggestions; can be trained in-house or done by J-SAT coders.	Evaluates multiple treatment and therapy interventions; easier to code than the MISC; good to excellent inter-rater reliability on YACS II items; potential for shorter training on 9 MI items only.
Intensive training; inter-rater review sessions are time consuming; provides no data on client change talk.	Intensive training; inter-rater review sessions are time consuming; provides no data on client change talk.	No additional videos for testing agent gain scores; written responses provide less information about agents' skills than tapes of sessions; no measure of client change talk.	Intensive training; inter-rater review sessions are time consuming; requires competency in providing written feedback and using Microsoft Excel software.	Primarily intended for research; potentially intensive training; inter-rater review sessions are time consuming; lack of validation on MI items; provides no data on client change talk.

EXHIBIT 4–6: GLOBAL MEASURES AND BEHAVIOR COUNTS IN MI INTERVIEW TAPE EVALUATION SYSTEMS

Interviewer Global and Likert Scale Measures

	BECCI 2.0	MISC 1.0	MISC 2.5	CLAMI	MITI 2.0	MITI 3.0	VASC	YACS II
Acceptance								
Acknowledging challenges								
Affirming strengths								
Change planning								
Collaboration								
Direction								
Egalitarianism								
Elicitation of motivation to change								
Empathy								
Evocation								
Exploring ambivalence								
Genuineness								
Heightening discrepancies								
MI Spirit/Style								
Summarizing								
Supporting client autonomy								
Warmth								

Relationship Measures:

	BECCI 2.0	MISC 1.0	MISC 2.5	CLAMI	MITI 2.0	MITI 3.0	VASC	YACS II
Benefit								
Collaboration								

Interviewer Behavior Counts

	BECCI 2.0	MISC 1.0	MISC 2.5	CLAMI	MITI 2.0	MITI 3.0	VASC	YACS II
Advising								
Affirming								
Asking closed questions								
Asking open questions								
Confronting								
Directing								
Emphasizing client control								
Facilitating								
Giving information								
MI Adherent								
MI Non-Adherent								
Offering personal feedback								
Paraphrasing								
Providing a complex reflection								
Providing a simple reflection								
Providing filler								
Providing structure								
Raising concern								
Reframing								
Rephrasing								
Self-disclosing								
Summarizing								
Supporting								
Warning								

Client Global and Likert Scale Measures

	BECCI 2.0	MISC 1.0	MISC 2.5	CLAMI	MITI 2.0	MITI 3.0	VASC	YACS II
Affect								
Cooperation								
Disclosure								
Engagement								
Resistance								
Self-exploration								

Client Behavior Counts

Change Talk:

	BECCI 2.0	MISC 1.0	MISC 2.5	CLAMI	MITI 2.0	MITI 3.0	VASC	YACS II
Expressing a desire to change								
Expressing a need to change								
Expressing ability to optimism for change								
Expressing commitment to change								
Expressing concern about the status quo								
Other movement toward change								
Providing reasons to change								
Recognizing a problem								
Reporting steps taken toward change								

Sustain Talk:

	BECCI 2.0	MISC 1.0	MISC 2.5	CLAMI	MITI 2.0	MITI 3.0	VASC	YACS II
Expressing a desire not to change								
Expressing a need not to change								
Expressing commitment not to change								
Expressing inability to change								
Other movement away from change								
Providing reasons not to change								
Reporting steps taken away from change								

Resistance:

	BECCI 2.0	MISC 1.0	MISC 2.5	CLAMI	MITI 2.0	MITI 3.0	VASC	YACS II
Arguing								
Interrupting								
Negating								
Not following								

Neutral:

	BECCI 2.0	MISC 1.0	MISC 2.5	CLAMI	MITI 2.0	MITI 3.0	VASC	YACS II
Asking a question								
Following								

■ = Included in system

☐ = Not included

then enter skill totals, global rankings, and written comments into reporting software. Software reports provide a graphed comparison of current and past agent averages, along with agency and national database skill percentage averages and rankings. Agent skill percentages are also converted into a "skill balance" score that summarizes overall adherence to the skill percentages recommended in MI literature. This balance provides an easy reference for determining gain scores from later tape submissions. As with the MITI, coder training involves manual reading and 30–40 hours of training, followed by periodic review sessions. Contractors and technical assistance are available to help agencies without the resources to train in-house raters. Contact the National Institute of Corrections at *www.nicic.gov* for more information.

Yale Adherence and Competence Scale–MI Items (YACS II-MI). The full YACS II tool provides Likert scale ratings for 69 staff skill evaluation items in the areas of conducting assessment, supporting clients, clinical management, 12-step facilitation, cognitive behavioral treatment, interpersonal therapy, motivational interviewing, and other supplemental tasks. Each item receives two 1–7 ratings: one for frequency and extensiveness of skill use and the other for skill level or competence. There are nine items specifically pertaining to MI, focusing on agent behaviors that roughly correspond to the basic principles and eight stages of learning MI. The YACS II does not assess client responses. Training involves manual reading, a seminar that reviews the manual and provides group rating experiences, completion of 10 followup practice rating tapes for inter-rater reliability, and regular followup sessions to correct drift from recommended scoring criteria. Training time might vary considerably, depending on whether agencies are training and practicing the full YACS II or just the nine MI items. Evaluations of the initial YACS (2000) tool showed excellent reliability and validity;[16, 17] the nine MI items were added in the YACS II, so they have not yet been independently validated. The tool and manual may be purchased from the Yale University School of Medicine at *http://web.med.yale.edu/ psych/research/psychotherapy/orderform.doc*.

Strategies for MI Evaluation

There are a variety of ways to accomplish MI evaluation depending on an agency's staff and monetary resources. Agencies with the resources to train their own staff in evaluation may contract with rating tool designers or other qualified trainers at the following websites to set up in-house staff trainings on using the various tools, providing written feedback, and offering followup skill coaching:

BECCI-CJ
Self-directed manual training only at
www.motivationalinterview.org/library

MISC, MITI, CLAMI, or Coaching Training
http://motivationalinterview.org/training/index.html

MITI, MISC 2.0, Feedback, and Coaching Training
www.j-sat.com/TrainingServices/ AssessmentInterviewCritiquerTraining.aspx

YACS Training
Order training manual and video from
http://web.med.yale.edu/psych/research/ psychotherapy/orderform.doc

Agencies with more limited resources may want to outsource their MI evaluation by shipping tapes of agent-client sessions to offsite consultants who provide evaluation, feedback, and coaching services by e-mail or phone:

MITI and CLAMI Tape Evaluation and/ or Coaching
info2@motivationalinterview.org

MITI and MISC 2.0 Tape Evaluation and/ or Coaching
www.j-sat.com/ManagementTools/TapeCritiques.aspx

YACS Tape Evaluation

joy.ortiz@yale.edu

Agencies may also choose a combination of these approaches, contracting with external providers to rate taped interactions and provide written feedback to staff supervisors onsite who have been trained to use this written feedback to provide skill coaching to their staff.

Both onsite training and offsite contracting options have pros and cons. Training staff to do evaluations, at minimum, would require:

- Procuring a tool manual.

- Providing staff the time to understand manual material through reading and 30–40 hours of training, depending on the tool.

- Holding regular evaluator meetings to help raters stay on the same page with their approach to rating various items.

- Allocating sufficient staff time for periodic skill rating and tool completion, providing both oral or written feedback to agents and followup agent coaching.

Adequate training and regular followup review sessions are key for maintaining the level of inter-rater reliability that allows feedback to be sufficiently accurate and meaningful for the agents being evaluated. So, if it is not possible to train and review sufficiently to keep staff on track, the usefulness of in-house evaluation will be undermined. In addition, managers would need to consider the relationships between the staff who are evaluating and those who are being evaluated. If an agency climate supports honest, constructive feedback, staff may feel okay rating each other honestly and the feedback and the evaluation process would not be compromised by the fear of offending a coworker. If the agency climate does not support this kind of interaction, honest evaluation may present a challenge.

If it is possible to overcome the resource and agency climate barriers to internal evaluation, the payoff for building this internal capacity would be:

- The potential for considerable skill improvements for staff who are trained in evaluation and coaching.

- The capacity to evaluate staff quickly and often, without shipping delays or fees from external providers.

- Possible increases in staff comfort because they are being evaluated by people with whom they are already familiar.

- The potential for changing agency norms about being evaluated. Because this process might occur much more frequently, it also increases the potential for staff to feel comfortable with exploring skill acquisition processes with colleagues and supervisors.

On the positive side, external evaluation can:

- Save agencies the hassle of staff training and followup inter-rater reliability sessions.

- Allow feedback and coaching to come from outside sources that are not involved in agency hierarchies or conflicting relational dynamics.

- Provide reasonable assurance that raters have been trained carefully in rating competencies and can maintain inter-rater reliability.

- Reduce the initial delays in evaluation that come from staff training.

- Save agencies the trouble of training new staff in evaluation as the originally trained staff change jobs or positions.

- Reduce the strain on staff workloads that comes from adding evaluation to the list of staff responsibilities.

External evaluation also has the downsides of:

- Not developing staff's skills in rating and coaching.

- Requiring procurement of funds whenever tapes are sent out for evaluation.

- Shipping delays.

- Rater lack of familiarity with agency norms, climate, constraints, and policies.

- Agent doubt in the validity of feedback from raters who are not part of the agency.

Policymakers and management staff will need to decide whether building internal capacity for skill rating and coaching or contracting with external providers best fits current agency resources, dynamics, and evaluation needs.

MI Evaluator Competencies

If agencies decide to build their own internal cadre of MI evaluators, there are several evaluator competencies they should consider in deciding which staff would best fulfill this function. Most MI raters can learn posttraining written assessments like the HRQ or the VASE-R fairly quickly and easily. While there may be nuances to scoring with these tools, the function of comparing written trainee responses to written MI manual criteria and assigning a numeric score remains consistent. However, with the evaluation of taped interviews, difficulty increases as additional types of agent and client skills are assessed. The cognitive and interpersonal skills that produce quality interview ratings and feedback are numerous and varied. Furthermore, tape evaluator trainers often find that about one-third of people who attend MI evaluation training are unable to maintain adequate inter-rater reliability standards for tools that include global measures and behavior counts.

Thus, agencies that want to develop their own local group of evaluators may improve the effectiveness of their evaluation training by assessing staff's degree of interest in learning MI evaluation and then prescreening trainees according to the kinds of competencies that they will be expected to develop. Managers may wish to consult staff supervisors, past performance reviews, resumes, or a variety of other sources to determine the likelihood that trained staff will be able to acquire the competencies necessary for the rating and coaching tasks assigned to them. The lists that follow suggest competencies that are helpful for certain types of assessment functions:

Competencies for Rating Global Measures and Likert Scales

- Maintaining competency in MI principles and theories.

- Maintaining familiarity with scale and rating definitions from relevant manuals.

- Considering both verbal and nonverbal cues in ratings.

- Understanding and adjusting for cultural and agency-setting variations in tone, proxemics, gestures, humor, and use of language.

- Adjusting for client dynamics that affect agent measures, and vice versa.

- Being aware of and adjusting for personal scoring tendencies (e.g., individual transference, being consistently too "generous" or "stingy").

- Differentiating between similar or overlapping concepts (e.g., acceptance vs. egalitarianism).

Competencies for Coding Client and Agent Behaviors

- Disassociating overall impressions of agent-client MI skills from definitions of particular behaviors.

- Disassociating client behaviors from agent behaviors to rate each separately.

- Maintaining familiarity with behavior category definitions and scoring rules.

- Tolerating ambiguity in behavior ratings.

- Self-correcting for categorizing tendencies that deviate from rating group norms.

- Maintaining focus on detailed communication for interviews lasting up to 90 minutes.

- Calculating sums, averages, and percentages for feedback.

Competencies for Providing Written Feedback to Agents

- Understanding ideal behavior percentages and global measure rankings.

- Finding genuine ways to reinforce all agents positively, even those with substandard skill demonstrations (50–80 percent of the feedback should be positive).

- Writing in clear language without MI or field jargon so agents can understand the rater's comments.

- Using MI theory in feedback suggestions, affirmations, and explanations.

- Modeling the MI spirit in constructive comments that avoid blaming, shaming, confronting, etc.

- Using specific examples and percentages that provide clear skill improvement targets.

- Giving agents the benefit of the doubt, rather than assuming.

Competencies for Providing Face-to-Face or Phone Feedback to Agents

- Explaining percentages, rankings, thresholds, and competency standards in clear, supportive terms.

- Not taking agent resistance or frustration personally.

- Being sensitive to job pressures and system constraints that impede agents' skill development abilities.

- Eliciting agent feedback about the process first.

- Empathetically reflecting agent ambivalence, difficulties, or concerns.

- Providing genuine affirmations before suggestions.

- Eliciting agent improvement goals before providing recommendations.

- Helping agents develop skill practice strategies.

Preparing for Successful MI Interview Evaluator Training

In addition to determining staff's readiness to learn MI evaluation and competencies for the task, there are several additional ways in which agencies may prepare for training ahead of time. These can help evaluators feel supported in difficult and time-consuming learning processes. Training planners may:

- Consult master schedules and budgets to ensure that trainees will have sufficient time and funding each month to complete their interview rating assignments, in addition to their other agency work.

- Schedule interview evaluation assignments on a monthly basis so that agents complete ratings regularly enough to maintain their skills.

- Provide trainees with evaluation manuals in advance of the training and arrange for rewards, pretraining tests, or other accountability measures to ensure that trainees read the manual indepth before the training.

- Provide sufficient training time, allowing agents to practice rating, explore their own ambivalence about rating tasks, and get all of their questions answered.

- Provide a sufficient number of posttraining practice tapes followed by coaching for raters, allowing them to work up to inter-rater reliability standards gradually.

- Train raters in providing written and face-to-face feedback in addition to rating interviews, and provide followup practices for them in this skill as well.

- Select a local staff person as the go-to person for coordinating interview tracking, distribution, and feedback processes.

- Plan for regular (weekly, monthly, or quarterly) followup review sessions for all trainees to correct drift and maintain inter-rater reliability standards.

- Plan to have all trainees rate the same tape at regular intervals (e.g., every 20th tape) to provide normative feedback to trainees about the areas in which they vary from the group.

While MI evaluation processes can appear daunting at first, especially when agencies are in the midst of deciding which tool to use, the individualized skill feedback that evaluation processes provide is essential for staff's progress toward on-the-job competence in MI. Without followup evaluation, the effects of training can only be short term and the potential for improved outcomes that MI research indicates will never be realized. Whether agencies decide to use simple Likert scale tools or more complex assessments of client and agent utterances completed by either internal or external raters, the key is that agencies move forward with the best evaluation solution that they can undertake at the present time. Additional training and more complicated assessment tools may follow eventually, but adopting a particular evaluation process and integrating it into the MI learning process lays the foundation for the eventual success of MI implementation.

Endnotes

1. W.R. Miller, C.E. Yahne, T. B. Moyers, J. Martinez, and M. Pirritanno, "A Randomized Trial of Methods to Help Clinicians Learn Motivational Interviewing," *Journal of Consulting and Clinical Psychology* 72(6):1050–62, 2004.

2. D. Fixsen, S.F. Naoom, K.A. Blase, R.M. Friedman, and F. Wallace, *Implementation Research: A Synthesis of the Literature* (Tampa, FL: University of South Florida, Louis de la Parte Florida Mental Health Institute, The National Implementation Research Network, 2005).

3. S.T. Walters, S.A. Matson, J.S. Baer, and D.M. Ziedonis, "Effectiveness of Workshop Training for Psychosocial Addiction Treatments: A Systematic Review," *Journal of Substance Abuse Treatment* 29(4):283–93, 2005.

4. B. Bogue, N. Campbell, M. Carey, E. Clawson, D. Faust, K. Florio, L. Joplin, G. Keiser, B. Wasson, and W. Woodward, *Implementing Evidence-Based Practice in Community Corrections: The Principles of Effective Intervention* (Washington, DC: U.S. Department of Justice, National Institute of Corrections, 2004).

5. S. Rollnick, W.R. Miller, and C.C. Butler, *Motivational Interviewing in Health Care: Helping Patients Change Behavior* (New York: The Guilford Press, 2008).

6. W.R. Miller, K.E. Hedrick, and D.R. Orlofsky, "The Helpful Responses Questionnaire: A Procedure for Measuring Therapeutic Empathy," *Journal of Clinical Psychology* 47(3):444–48, 1991.

7. W.R. Miller and K.A. Mount, "A Small Study of Training in Motivational Interviewing: Does One Workshop Change Clinician and Client Behavior?" *Behavioural and Cognitive Psychotherapy* 29(4):457–71, 2001.

8. D.B. Rosengren, J.S. Baer, B. Hartzler, C.W. Dunn, and E.A. Wells, "The Video Assessment of Simulated Encounters (VASE): Development and Validation of a Group-Administered Method for Evaluating Clinician Skills in Motivational Interviewing," *Drug and Alcohol Dependence* 79(3):321–30, 2005.

9. T.B. Moyers and T. Martin, "Therapist Influence on Client Language During Motivational Interviewing Sessions," *Journal of Substance Abuse Treatment* 30(3):245–51, 2006.

10. P.C. Amrhein, W.R. Miller, C.E. Yahne, M. Palmer, and L. Fulcher, "Client Commitment Language During Motivational Interviewing

Predicts Drug Use Outcomes," *Journal of Consulting and Clinical Psychology* 71(5):862–78, 2003.

11. C. Lane, M. Huws-Thomas, K. Hood, S. Rollnick, K. Edwards, and M. Robling, "Measuring Adaptations of Motivational Interviewing: The Development and Validation of the Behavior Change Counseling Index (BECCI)," *Patient Education and Counseling* 56(2):166–73, 2005.

12. T.B. Moyers and T. Martin, *Assessing the Integrity of Motivational Interviewing Interventions: Reliability of the Motivational Interviewing Skill Code* (Albuquerque, NM: British Association for Behavioral and Cognitive Psychotherapies, 2003).

13. J. De Jonge, G. Schippers, and C. Schaap, "The Motivational Interviewing Skill Code: Reliability and a Critical Appraisal," *Behavioural and Cognitive Psychotherapy* 33(3):285–98, 2005.

14. T.B. Moyers, T. Martin, J.K. Manuel, S. Hendrickson, and W.R. Miller, "Assessing Competence in the Use of Motivational Interviewing," *Journal of Substance Abuse Treatment* 28(1):19–26, 2005.

15. D.M. Tappin, C. McKay, D. McIntyre, W.H. Gilmour, S. Cowan, F. Crawford, F. Currie, and M.A. Lumsden, "A Practical Instrument to Document the Process of Motivational Interviewing," *Behavioural and Cognitive Psychotherapy* 28:17–32, 2000.

16. K.M. Carroll, C. Nich, R.L. Sifry, K.F. Nuro, T.L. Frankforter, S.A. Ball, L. Fenton, and B.J. Rounsaville, "A General System for Evaluating Therapist Adherence and Competence in Psychotherapy Research in the Addictions," *Drug Alcohol Dependencies* 57(3):225–38, 2000.

17. M.B. Madson, T.C. Campbell, D.E. Barrett, M.J. Brondino, and T.P. Melchart, "Development of the Motivational Interviewing Supervision and Training Scale," *Psychology of Addictive Behaviors* 19:303–10, 2005.

CHAPTER 5 | Planning To Help Individuals Develop MI Skills in a Correctional Setting

Variations on the dialogue below have been a common occurrence in corrections for the past several years. It reflects a trend that might be cause for optimism as well as concern.

Caller
Hello, my agency wants to adopt motivational interviewing, and the National Institute of Corrections referred us to you as one of several reliable training agencies that could train us in the method. Is this something you might help us with?

Independent Contractor
Yes. We've been doing a fair amount of work helping different jurisdictions train their staff in MI. What makes your agency interested in MI?

Caller
Well, we're really into EBP. We've implemented the _____ (LSI-R; COMPAS; RAIS; ROPE; LS/CMI) assessment, individual case plans, and cog groups, and now we're ready to get trained in MI. The deputy director wants everyone trained before the end of the year.

Corrections systems are now gravitating toward motivational interviewing (MI)[1] in the same way that the addictions, mental health, and health-care fields continue to move into broader implementation of MI. However, unlike these other disciplines, corrections systems are paramilitary in nature. As such, they have a strong command-and-control background and orientation. When corrections systems adopt an innovation, it is often on scales larger than those of an agency of individual therapists or private primary care practitioners. The good news is that if a corrections system is successful in bringing an innovation or practice to scale, it will be widespread.

The not-so-good news is that there may be considerable barriers and obstacles to successful integration of these subtle, often complex, skills. MI is not an innovation that lends itself to being implemented by conventional methods, where an agency trains staff, then follows the training with just one quality assurance (QA) intervention (such as tape critiquing) and assumes that everybody is now practicing MI.

Learning MI takes practice, effort, feedback, and coaching.[2–4] Training is optional, due in part to the complex nature of the technical skills that comprise MI's seven or eight stages of learning or learning tasks. In addition, there is the crucial spirit of MI that deals with one's manner of being—how positively respectful one is in his/her interactions with others.[5, 6] This aspect of MI is something that can only develop in an individual over time. Learning MI is a lifelong enterprise in which someone is continually improving his/her interpersonal skills and ability to help others draw out their own solutions. Consequently, some alternative strategies to standard corrections training procedures appear promising for helping corrections staff sufficiently learn MI so that they are routinely and flexibly using this style in both neutral as well as heated interpersonal situations.

A key to delineating effective approaches for introducing and promoting MI skills within corrections is the perspective of the line agent. While line agents are notorious for having diverse and differing perspectives[7–9]—particularly with regard to sanctioning philosophies[10–12]—regarding their work, some predictable growth and segmentation generally takes place. Agents' motivation for adopting a complex skill set such as MI may shift according to their stage of career evolution, as well as the particular context or unit in which they are working. It may be worthwhile, therefore, to consider three common yet potentially pivotal "stations" that agents might hold over the course of their careers:

1. Staff newly recruited and hired.

2. Staff established in their jobs who are *not* interested in MI.

3. Staff established in their jobs who are interested in MI.

Tailoring MI training and support of skill development for each of these stations could provide a means for reducing push-back and generating genuine agent interest more readily than a standard, systemwide rollout approach.

This chapter examines the unique training opportunities that exist between new hires and veteran staff. Training new recruits entails high-leverage opportunities. A modest modification in attitudes, beliefs, and values at the onset of one's career can result in significantly different outcomes later.

In a paramilitary system such as corrections, not everyone advances into management ranks; most will remain at the line level for their entire career. This potential career stagnation can lead to employee issues regarding motivation, job fulfillment, and self-worth—a significant hindrance to working with a nonvoluntary population with considerable disorders of their own. Some of the more prevalent issues include agent burnout or emotional exhaustion,[13, 14] work orientations unaligned with any legitimate mission,[15–19] and a tendency toward insularity and "group think."[20] Such a culture—with accompanying mindsets—does not lend itself to becoming a learning organization[20–23] in or out of the training room. As such, many of these agents may not have strong incentives or simply cannot be bothered to learn innovations and skill sets such as MI.

Conversely, the option for becoming so engaged in one's work that it becomes a "calling" rather than a career does exist.[24] This engagement—where personal interest, aptitude, and values intersect around a particular strategy—can become a passion, quite the opposite of and possibly the antidote to the syndromes that can emerge out of career stagnation. Fortunately, a fair amount of staff always appear to have a natural interest in learning the latest evidence-based practices such as MI.[25] These agents, who find themselves energized by new and evolving practices and job skills, present another unique kind of training and staff development challenge.

Introducing MI to Newly Recruited Staff

Upon hiring, most new agents are arguably more impressionable than at any other point in their subsequent career. Probation and parole officers typically have a bachelor's degree based in the social sciences. Correctional officers more often have a high school diploma, possibly accompanied by some additional college coursework. This level of education provides the new agent with only rudimentary knowledge about the criminal justice system and even less insight regarding the psychology of criminal behavior.[26]

If young, these new agents probably do not have much life experience in general, and in particular, little (if any) experience working with offenders. In fact, most of their impressions and images of offenders likely come from media sources that tend to glamorize crime and deviance. As young agents enter the field and assume caseloads or shifts, they will be introduced to a culture of veteran staff who have transitioned from being inexperienced in working with offenders themselves to being inordinately experienced—in certain ways. Compared to the average citizen, experienced corrections staff have many thousands more interactions with different offenders. Given the challenge of interacting with a relatively risky, unknown offender population, and the discrepancy between their own direct experience at this task and the experience of their coworkers, it is natural that new recruits quickly learn to defer to the expertise of their more experienced colleagues. In doing so, new agents adopt existing norms, mental models, and practices.[22, 27] Thus, a seamless process for reproducing the culture of corrections exists naturally. What could be wrong with this? Nothing if there were no attempts at innovation in the field.

The introduction of more complex skill sets such as MI and cognitive behavioral treatment requires support and commitment from personnel, including a shift in collegial norms.[28] Innovative practices that promote transparency of practice, reciprocal or peer coaching, recognition of expertise, and encourage feedback[29] are helpful and ultimately required if staff are to develop proficiency in MI. However, these practices often run against the grain of typical correctional norms that do not promote transparency with respect to staff interaction during coaching and counseling of offenders. More typically, it is an unstated policy that interactions that go on behind closed doors with another agent's caseload are nobody else's business. This kind of tacit understanding can undermine opportunities for learning complex skills such as MI by discouraging natural feedback and coaching opportunities.

Other established and conventional norms can provide additional barriers to learning sensitive communication skills. Mental models[30, 31] that convey the notion that offenders have questionable humanity, or that they have few solutions within themselves, interfere with engaging offenders as equals who have tremendous inner potential for overcoming problems. Norms that extol staff as tough-minded versus compassionate, or cynical rather than open-minded, can be pervasive and problematic. While perhaps novel and provocative for new staff, these models and norms can thwart their efforts to explore their own perspectives due to environmental workplace pressure to adopt existing norms. In short, established norms

and emerging relationships that new hires form with veteran agents have the potential to inhibit learning and curtail real growth and development. Due to the effect that the existing culture may have on new recruits, providing them with a sound logic and vision for their job,[32] preservice training with subsequent attention to communities of practice, and followup coaching is vital to their ongoing success.

Providing newly recruited staff a comprehensive indoctrination in the business, law enforcement, and offender case management processes is paramount for launching their careers on the best possible track.[33] Ideally, if new hires receive thorough training prior to their first exposure to coworkers or offenders, they will have the chance to form mental models consistent with the preferred manner of doing business.

Effective pre-service training should incorporate adequate follow-through that assures the application of skills in correctional settings that are very dissimilar from the classroom (*far transfer*).[34] The follow-through may include not only booster training, formal feedback, and coaching opportunities, but also links to advisers and mentors, as well as naturally forming communities of practice. Taken together, these mechanisms can provide a sufficient structure to isolate staff long enough for them to become adequately familiar with the core components and logic of their system's primary strategies for supervision. Equally important, this extensive developmental period will allow new staff to practice and "overlearn" new fundamental skills, such as active listening, so that they are no longer self-conscious in applying their new skills when they enter the real world of their jobs.

Incorporating MI Skill Development Into Pre-Service Training

Setting Clear, Logical, and Inspiring Expectations

MI does not operate in a vacuum, but rather in the context of a dynamic, complex, and highly interactive environment. Therefore, it is extremely helpful to map out for new hires the why, what, and how of their new job. This map needs to include a description of all the components of a position as well as the underlying logic connecting these components and their mutual interactions. The most efficient way to convey the map is through a logic model, a diagram that visually depicts the logic between system inputs, activities, outputs, and outcomes.[35, 36] However, logic models require technical thinking,[37] and most correctional systems are only beginning to understand the value and methods for maintaining them.[38, 39] More typically, correctional systems have formulated policies and procedures (P&P), and these tend to conceal the overarching logic and strategies by which an organization intends to obtain good outcomes. P&P also sacrifice a great deal of descriptive meaning about the relationships between the components. As EBP

advances into correctional practice, it will behoove leaders to see to it that new recruits understand from the onset of their careers not only what it is they are expected to do to support these EBP (along with why, and how to go about doing it), but what the relationship is between the various EBP and core practices.

Forming a logic model requires a working group of stakeholders with a willingness to think hard and long for a series of two to three half-day sessions. Groups can format their logic model in different styles coinciding with the purpose or intended use of the model.[37] A number of free resources are available on the Internet for guiding this process. Exhibit 5–1 is an example of a logic model specifically for corrections that includes MI components.

EXHIBIT 5-1: SAMPLE LOGIC MODEL USING MI COMPONENTS

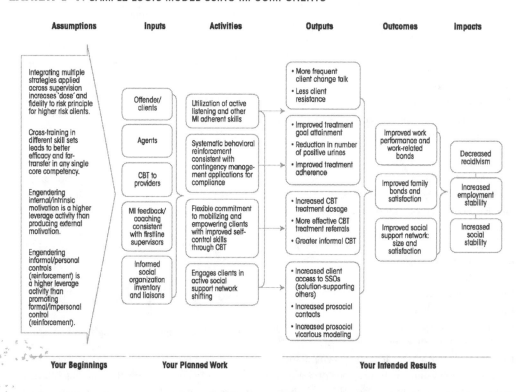

Overlearning in Preservice Training

The *eight-task model*[40] that delineates the key learning skills necessary for becoming proficient in MI (see *Exercises for Developing MI Skills in Corrections*) is also pertinent for identifying crucial MI training elements in preservice training for newly hired staff. According to the authors of *Motivational Interviewing: Preparing People to Change* (Miller and Rollnick)[5] the four core principles of MI are:

1. Aiding the individual in *developing discrepancy* related to a target behavior.

2. *Expressing empathy* via client-centered or active listening skills.

3. *Rolling with resistance* rather than directly opposing it.

4. *Supporting self-efficacy* for the target behavior(s).

Moreover, in a recent review of the research on training MI, Madson[41] and his colleagues suggest that four of the eight tasks of learning MI are most directly related to the principles. Consequently, the preferred focus for providing a foundational introductory training to MI is one that includes a fair amount of experiential training in:

- Learning the spirit of MI.

- Acquiring active listening skills.

- Learning to identify and reinforce change talk in others.

- Working with resistance so that this energy can be applied to change.

In the case of training new recruits, it will be important to give equal emphasis to both *real plays,* or real-world experiences, and role plays in preservice training. Real plays invite recruits to use their own life experiences, feelings, and beliefs in structured interactions where one student practices his/her skills with another. This allows for more realistic, real-time cues, while recruits

experience firsthand how the use of MI skills can affect people. Role plays, on the other hand, allow recruits to practice context-specific scenarios most relevant to their new work setting (e.g., doing assessments in an intake and diagnostic facility or setting up case plans in a probation or parole unit). If possible, it is also advantageous to use prepared offender actors as well to ensure that participant recruits finish the training with increased efficacy about using MI skills with offenders. Training the above skill tasks ideally involves *scaffolding,* where exercises focusing on a particular skill begin first with elementary skills (e.g., simple reflections) and build upon them and graduate to more complex skill combinations (e.g., *agreement with a twist* that deliberately combines a reflection with a *reframe*) later.

Training programs that incorporate the classic "tell-show-try" sequence for training behavioral skills appear to be a favorite for training MI in general. There should be no exception for preservice training. The latter cycle of behavioral training emphasizes the "try" phase by encouraging slightly redundant but diverse exercise drills that can take place in dyads, triads, quads, "fishbowls," or with the entire training group. Repetition and variety are the touchstones for having sufficient skill rehearsals to support far transfer to the work setting.

It is critical for several reasons that the trainers are able to demonstrate examples of each skill in a variety of ways. First, having adequate models helps guide the participant's efforts and approximations to have fidelity with the new skills. Second, with new recruits there is the potential for powerful vicarious reinforcement through seeing someone who has deeper experience in managing offenders effectively modeling the skills and obtaining the desired effects in his/her interactions. Third, when trainers possess the necessary MI style and skills, they can flexibly accommodate demands from novice participants for impromptu demonstrations at various points in the training when participants forget or want to refine a basic skill. Finally, quite often when training MI, the modeling involves responding to the training participants themselves, in an MI-adherent manner[41] that consistently draws out the participants' best motivation, attitudes, and solutions. Having trainers who are competent in MI may present initial challenges if academy-type training is delivered primarily by full-time trainers who lack clinical experience with MI.

Ideally, training curriculums for MI include a large amount of flexibility in order to adapt to different emerging group themes and agendas. This flexibility can be vital to stretch and fit across the wide variety of perspectives, values, and aptitudes one can generally anticipate in any cross-section of corrections staff. However, with new recruits, there may be some value in structuring the curriculum in sequences to facilitate their ability to integrate new micro-skills into a larger, emerging picture of what their new roles will look like within the corrections enterprise they are beginning to understand.

Communities of Practice

Communities of Practice (CoP)[42, 43] is both a sociological and business term describing how loosely and informally configured groups of people perform and promote learning among themselves. While they are everywhere, CoP do not necessarily conform to any certain team, set, unit, or sector. All that is required to qualify is:

1. A joint enterprise (e.g., we are bringing EBP into our agency).

2. A shared repertoire of skills.

3. Mutual engagement (where hierarchy norms can be suspended).

See exhibit 5–2 for a visual representation of this model.

Healthy CoP help members exchange new meanings about their work and who they are; they act

EXHIBIT 5-2: THE THREE ELEMENTS IN A COMMUNITY OF PRACTICE

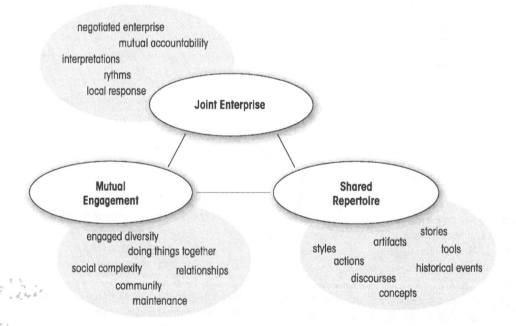

Source: E. Wenger, *Communities of Practice: Learning, Meaning, and Identity* (New York: Cambridge University Press, 1998).

as mini-parallel learning organizations and contain rich potential coaching resources. Peer and expert coaching is most efficient when it takes place locally, within one's own indigenous CoP. This requires sufficiently strong feedback norms where peers and experts feel comfortable providing feedback and coaching to each other.

Every time a new recruit cohort arises, based on the informal ties that take place, there is the potential for a slightly new and different CoP to enter and/or emerge in the organization. This may represent a somewhat unique opportunity for introducing productive norms for achieving the agency's mission. Small group or breakout sessions in the training that encourage collective cost-benefit thinking around innovations such as MI and other EBP can begin to instill a sense of shared enterprise and skills. They can also reinforce reciprocating engagement and support between staff. When trust and mutual respect are fostered, it makes staff feel more comfortable adopting new values, considering new perspectives, and practicing fragile new MI skills with greater earnestness and determination.

Advisers, Coaches, and Mentors

There is fascinating literature that goes into great detail delineating the differences and distinctions between advisers, coaches, and mentors.[44-46] People performing these roles can be measured by two categories: degree of engagement and expertise. Advisers can advise with little of either; coaches need a modicum of both; and mentors can and will draw deeply upon each of these resources. Individuals in these roles tend to serve and facilitate growth and learning in others. How can this be more consciously coordinated?

The interpersonal connections that are taking place as new hires infiltrate their new organization are inevitable and may have tremendous influence on the new hires' subsequent careers. Preservice MI training that more deliberately facilitates the alignments new recruits make with advisers, coaches, and mentors invariably results in greater far transfer. The trick is making these potential connections more transparent.

Anyone who knows the workings of an organization can be an adviser. All that is necessary is an assignment that assures that the new hire has an opportunity to avail himself/herself of someone willing and able to advise him/her on what to prioritize, when to do things, and where to go with it all. In its most perfunctory aspect, an adviser performs as a traffic cop: an extremely helpful but ultimately superficial role that enables new hires to get from point A to B (or C, etc.) as they are starting their careers. Identifying and assigning advisers to new recruits for their first 6–9 months on the job will have the benefit of:

- Tapping all able veteran staff to be in a unique and useful role, giving to someone else word-of-mouth insights they themselves have received over their careers.

- Making an informed "generalist" available and accessible to all new recruits in order to help them quickly orientate and get them off to the best possible start.

- Give the new hires an advantage in finding and meeting a coach who is right for them, one whom they can consult according to their own priorities.

Notwithstanding buddy or peer coaching, the role of a coach requires some expertise in a given area. In corrections, many staff are qualified to coach on many things (e.g., evidence chain of custody, assessment protocols, firearms, cognitive behavioral training (CBT) curriculums or individual coaching, and MI). What helps is getting people qualified and getting qualified people certified (or at least inventoried) so that the resources they possess might be mobilized. There is no substitute for having an adequate pool of skill-specific coaches. Once appropriate skill-specific coaches are inventoried based on some thresholds for proficiency, a system is well on its way toward becoming more transparent, friendly to navigate, and coach-ready.

As mentioned earlier, one of an adviser's primary tasks is to assist other staff in meeting coaches. Every local agency has an informal or formal inventory of staff qualified to provide coaching in various skill sets. It is the responsibility of the local advisers to maintain and keep this local inventory current so they can expedite referrals when necessary.

When are referrals to MI coaches most helpful? Referrals are preferably made during or immediately after preservice training, before the half-life of skills learned in an artificial classroom begins to expire. An individual's MI coach will be the best person to guide him/her in the timing of tape recording data collection for formal MI skill feedback. Later, coaches will also be in the best position to determine which staff qualify for additional training (e.g., advanced MI skills, peer MI coaching), by demonstrating minimal MI skill proficiency threshold performance (e.g., **MITI-3** criteria such as 1:1 reflections-to-questions ratio). In this manner, the MI support system becomes self-sustaining.

Finally, there are mentors.[47] As mentioned earlier, the bar gets set higher for mentors in many respects. First, anything short of a mutually voluntary relationship never works. The principle is attraction; somebody has something (a set of skills and attributes) somebody else wants, and the first person wants to share it. Second, the threshold level of proficiency goes beyond the journeyman level for coaches to that of "master," or certifiable proficiency across an array of measures, for mentors. Third, mentor-protégé relationships are complex, developmental, and symbiotic.[48, 49] To enter into and maintain this type of relationship has tremendous value for somebody's career as well as the host organization.[50] As such, this type of extracurricular activity might be formally reinforced, but extrinsic rewards are more than likely to be superfluous given the personal nature of the relationship. What an agency can do is make the possibility apparent by identifying active mentors and providing an assortment of current testimony from protégés and mentors.

Introducing MI to Established Staff Who Are *Not* Interested in Learning MI

There are several reasons to revisit the wisdom of strategies to bring MI skills into a corrections system via a *mandatory* training rollout. Learning MI takes time and personal commitment, neither of which comes out of a conventional rollout. Research has determined that training is basically a noncritical event; feedback and coaching, on the other hand, are essential. It also appears that a large portion (30 percent) of practitioners in all fields where MI has been trained (e.g., addictions treatment, the mental health and the broader medical health fields) are not going to learn MI,[51] either because of capacity or lack of interest. In addition, the very nature of a nonvoluntary training strategy is at odds with the spirit of MI.[52]

The spirit of MI tells us all people share a rich human potential. People make their best efforts to change when the motivation comes from within, and maintaining one's autonomy of choice—the notion that people ultimately decide for themselves whether they will change a given behavior—is a universal and important attribute of being human. Consequently, when staff tell their managers that they are not interested in learning any "touchy-feely" MI skills, and management responds, "Attend the training anyway—it is mandatory," there is apt to be a conflict and split with some of the core principles of MI at the very onset of the rollout.

In order to learn the technical aspects of MI, an individual has to be able to do three things very quickly, almost simultaneously:

1. Visualize the verbal report they are receiving from whomever they are chatting with.

2. Transform that report into a hypothesis regarding what the larger scope of feelings, thoughts, and meanings is for the individuals expressing themselves.

3. Express that hypothesis in the form of a conversational statement in real time.

This can be a very tall order, particularly if one is experiencing some personal distress of his/her own, is an especially concrete thinker, or is extremely self-centered.

In terms of the nontechnical or spirit dimensions of MI, low self-esteem may present significant constraints to learning and adopting MI, insofar as it can be very challenging for people who have difficulties accepting themselves to accept the people they are interviewing or with whom they are conversing.[29]

Taken together, the above constraints to learning both the technical and nontechnical dimensions of MI present a reality that is seldom considered once a rollout strategy has begun to unfold. Under the best circumstances (e.g., with followup feedback and coaching), only about 70 percent of the participants will be ready, willing, and able to learn MI.[51] This sobering math brings into question the return on investment (ROI) for MI training rollout strategies in corrections. Moreover, if one considers the "braking effect" that reluctant or incapable learners have on other participants in a typical training, there is more cause to be skeptical about rolling out training systemwide.

Finally, it is very difficult to assure that all participants in a rollout situation will have the time, commitment, and prerequisite feedback/coaching to ensure success. These resources are essential so that trainees can practice and develop their MI skills to either the "process" or "performance" levels, beyond a mere "paper" implementation. However, it is much easier to mobilize these resources under a pilot condition, and even more workable to do so when staff have some initial motivation for learning MI in the first place.

Consequently, the preferred alternative to a mandatory rollout training in MI is for staff who are not interested enough in MI to volunteer (for training, tape feedback, and coaching) to simply help provide information to those who are. Such an awareness-building campaign might involve an afternoon in-service session or a larger-audience format with an overview presentation. Hopefully,

these sessions will be accompanied by testimonials from officers who have elected to get on the path of learning MI and have begun to enjoy some of the benefits of their efforts. Sometimes, encouraging unmotivated staff to attend small group brainstorm exercises (such as a SWOT (Strengths, Weakness, Opportunities, and Threats), multivote, or cause-and-effect diagramming) toward the end of the overview can help create some new thinking and attitudes. Whenever staff previously unmotivated to learn MI change their minds, they should be welcome to submit applications to attend a full 3-day basic MI training.

Introducing MI to Established Staff Who *Are* Interested in Learning MI

If the MI skill development of new hires has been addressed from the onset of their careers, and the MI skill development for established staff who are not yet interested is for the most part left up to their discretion, the personnel left in an organization are established staff who *are* motivated to enter an MI training program. These staff may be motivated, first to develop their ability to learn MI and second, to begin an ongoing process of practice and learning in order to cultivate singular and powerful interpersonal skills throughout their career. The manner in which these valuable staff are recruited into training and introduced to MI through subsequent training and followup is crucial.

Pilot Initiatives

Establishing an initial, well-planned pilot for basic introductory training in MI for interested staff is a great way to start. In business, piloting innovations prior to rolling them out is standard practice.[53] However, in human services, new legislation often moves immediately into systemwide implementation. Considerable advantages appear to piloting a new implementation versus implementing it to scale.[54] Some of the advantages of piloting are:

- Creating a deliberate "selection effect" for who is to be involved in the initial implementation and where it will take place.

- Identifying problems not previously anticipated and subsequently avoiding multiplier effects of these problems in the ensuing full implementation.

- Identifying opportunities not previously anticipated and subsequently creating positive multiplier effects in the rollout implementation.

- Assuring that fewer resources will be wasted in the full implementation by first assembling, coordinating, and aligning on a small scale all the necessary drivers for success.

A pilot design can be initiated in a variety of manners. Assuming that interest and willingness to be trained is already a given selection criteria, an agency can select a specific region, unit, or sector (e.g., intake/presentence investigation officers versus supervision). In addition, a pilot can be executed by selecting participants based on certain individual characteristics—e.g., good self-esteem or interest in helping clients resolve their ambivalence for change (there are surveys or tests in the appendix that measure both). Piloting on select staff attributes can also be complemented by using a regional "sampling frame" so that a set quota of staff (e.g., 2–4) can be selected from each region or district in a system. This combines the advantages of having a relatively diffuse implementation with a smaller scale and decidedly positive individual staff selection effects (though it undoubtedly increases the logistic complications and costs).

Implementation Planning

Formulating an implementation plan prior to the onset of the pilot implementation will generally pay dividends well beyond the time and resources it costs to develop such a plan. Implementing MI successfully at a system level requires behavior change at the agent, firstline supervisor, and administrative support levels.[55–57] When it comes to implementation, there is a new sheriff in town—

implementation science[55]—and corrections planners would do well to review the basic principles for incorporating it into their respective plans. It could be particularly helpful to identify and examine what some of the classic drivers are for effective implementation:

- **Practice-based practitioner selection.** Select staff with practice records that are in alignment with the (MI) innovation.

- **Preservice and inservice skill-based training.** Provide training prior to implementing the innovation as well as during and throughout the implementation.

- **Practice-based coaching and ongoing consultation.** Provide coaching opportunities in a variety of manners (e.g., individual, group, formal, impromptu) that concentrate on everyday corrections MI skill sets.

- **Staff evaluation and program evaluation.** Provide periodic, formal, and objective feedback to both the individual staff and the program or unit they are working within.

- **Facilitative administrative support.** Arrange for flexible and timely leadership support, data transfer, reinforcement, and organizational assistance.

- **System collaboration and intervention.** Engage in ongoing collaboration with other related systems for greater stability, broader perspectives, and access to resources.

The drivers enumerated above are part of an emerging model for building overall implementation capacity in human services, where EBPs are becoming prevalent within and challenging many systems. These drivers and other tenets in the broader implementation research are congruent with the more specific emerging experimental studies focusing on training MI[2, 3, 41, 58] that have found feedback and coaching to be critical in developing MI skills. Formulating a plan based on these six drivers is in the interest of every MI implementation in corrections.

ORGANIZING MI TRAINING IMPLEMENTATION BASED ON IMPLEMENTATION DRIVERS

Here is an outline for implementing MI training and coaching that uses both implementation drivers and an inventory of recommendations for new recruits. This outline is a framework for creating a more concrete and specific implementation plan for developing staff MI skills (on a semivoluntary basis) in a correctional setting. At the same time, it might also be built out and elaborated upon as new mechanisms and better drivers for MI implementation are identified. It is a generic model that draws upon William Miller's often-repeated recommendation that in large bureaucracies, such as corrections, there may be real and lasting advantages to developing high-quality MI skills in a few individuals, as opposed to mediocre skills in many. (See exhibit 5–3 for a visual representation of the framework.)

1. **Practice-based staff selection**

   Try to delineate staff according to their current capacities, skills, and motivation to practice MI and apply training, coaching, and other resources accordingly.

   a. New recruits share an obligation to become familiar with the mission, values, and prevailing strategies of the organization that has recently hired them. It is incumbent upon the hiring agency to provide early and adequate initial training in the interventions it prioritizes or highlights as mission-critical, i.e., sensitive and constructive communication skills such as MI.

   b. Current staff not motivated to participate in MI training could benefit themselves and the agency by attending a brief information-sharing overview on MI. This will allow staff to identify and subsequently communicate some of the fundamental factors related to MI without being obligated to attend a skills-based training.

   c. Current staff motivated to participate in training and coaching processes for learning MI can apply through a prescribed selection process to become involved in a pilot project that has the potential for ultimately expanding into a full rollout for staff interested in acquiring MI skills. In addition to interest, and possibly staff location, there may be other possible criteria for screening (e.g., preference for training firstline supervisors first, performance evaluations related to good case worker skills, previously demonstrated aptitude for CBT or other EBP).

2. **Preservice and inservice skill-based training**

   a. New recruits undergo a 2- to 3-day training in MI that focuses on skills and values related to MI's four core principles. Training is highly experiential with minimal background and conceptual material. Peer coaching during the training is promoted and reinforced. Posttraining plans for ongoing skill development are emphasized and pre-/posttest and interim classroom skill ratings are recorded and maintained. All training program graduates are expected to turn in a 30- to 40-minute audiotape of themselves conducting an assessment followup session demonstrating their MI skills within 20 working days. This tape is critiqued by qualified MI skill raters using the Motivational Interviewing Therapeutic Integrity scale, 3d version (MITI-3). A full written report is formulated and transmitted to the participant within 10 working days of receipt of the tape.

   b. Staff *not* interested in MI are not provided skill-based training during inservice training, but instead they attend some form of a 2- to 3-hour informational MI overview followed by coordinated small group discussions.

   c. Staff interested in MI receive the identical MI basic training package that new recruits do with one exception: they are provided a set of preconference reading materials and a video along with an open book quiz. In addition to the initial MI training, established staff volunteering for MI are eligible for subsequent training in MI QA (MI skill rating and providing feedback), MI coaching, and training for trainers in MI.

3. **Practice-based coaching and ongoing consultation**

   a. New recruits are assigned both an adviser (any experienced staff or staff members who have demonstrated proficiency in at least one or more EBP, e.g., CBT, relapse prevention (RP), Contingency Management, MI) and an MI coach. The primary role of the adviser is to help new recruits connect to the resources, MI quality circles, and coaches and available mentors they need to get thoroughly oriented and established. Advisers are employed for 6 months. The MI coaches are local agents who have completed the full basic MI training package, including the followup tape critiquing and coaching, and demonstrated proficiency at minimal thresholds. Coaches help recently trained MI staff interpret their MI tape critique feedback reports and periodically practice (by modeling, real plays, and role plays).

whatever MI skill applications the novice finds interesting and challenging. Coaches also encourage and assist agents in establishing their own written MI skill development plans.

b. Staff not interested in MI are not provided with coaching or consultations, nor are they involved with any other subsequent implementation driver steps.

c. Staff interested in MI receive coaching and consultation identical to new recruits except that, in the initial stages of the training program, they use external or independent coaches who have been outsourced.

4. **Staff evaluations and program evaluations**

a. Both new recruits and established staff interested in learning MI receive direct observation of their supervision or intake contacts, with ratings using tools designed for quick measures, such as the Quality Contact Scale (QCS) or the MITI-3. These onsite observations and ratings are performed by any qualified staff (trained in rating and feedback), usually either MI coaches or firstline supervisors. Thereafter, at least two onsite client session observations are obtained per year for all trained staff, with feedback from all observations attached (if not integrated into each staff member's MI skill development plan).

b. Program evaluations consist of a biannual aggregation of all local unit agents' feedback measures (MITI-3), formulated as normative feedback reports that compare all local units' progress and evolution.

5. **Facilitative administrative support**

a. All MI-trained and -coached staff have a right to have access to support, peer coaching, and ongoing formal MI coaching. The latter support may take on a variety of unique local forms (e.g., MI quality circles or CoP; informal or routine MI practice sessions, clinical supervision sessions [outsourced or internal]). Barriers to these resources need to be inventoried routinely so that respective remedies can be immediately devised.

b. Incentive systems may need to be created to help trained staff maintain focus and commitment to MI skill development. Norms and thresholds for eligibility to QA and coaching workshops should be established by an MI implementation steering group, enlisted at the onset of the MI implementation project. In addition, the steering group should ratify the MI implementation plan.

c. Workload credits need to be applied for agents performing as coaches at various levels. Agents who have achieved multiple coaching statuses are automatically eligible for training of trainers for MI workshops. Agents working as part-time trainers should also get an additional workload credit. Those part-time trainers with the best evaluations and pre-/postgain scores should be eligible for Motivational Interviewing Network of Trainers (MINT) Training for New Trainers (TNT) in and out of the United States. (If funding is an issue, technical assistance can be applied for through the National Institute of Corrections.)

d. Firstline supervisors need to be prioritized for MI basic training to the extent that they are interested and willingly volunteer. Once supervisors have completed this preparatory phase, they should be offered specialized training, independent from coaching training, in how to teach new skills, strengthen confidence, provide a safe supervision session environment, and provide discipline for the specific skills[56] with which their subordinates struggle. In addition, there may be added benefits in training supervisors on how to help promote individual transparency, organizational mindfulness, and resiliency—the qualities of a learning organization.

6. **System collaboration and intervention**

a. MI implementation stakeholders (e.g., mental health and alcohol and other drug treatment providers, judges, parole board officials, offender family members, downstream corrections agencies, local college criminal justice departments, and sister agency recruitment grounds) can be inventoried and invited to the table—given minimally the same information that MI-disinterested staff receive—and placed in similar coordinated small group discussions. This emergent community of stakeholders can be harnessed for a variety of input, guidance, and potential new economies of scale (bringing in special trainers or consultants, purchasing bulk training materials, broadly showcasing achievements, and more strongly reinforcing unit or individual MI-related achievements).

EXHIBIT 5-3: EXAMPLE OF STRUCTURAL FRAMEWORK FOR IMPLEMENTATION CAPACITY

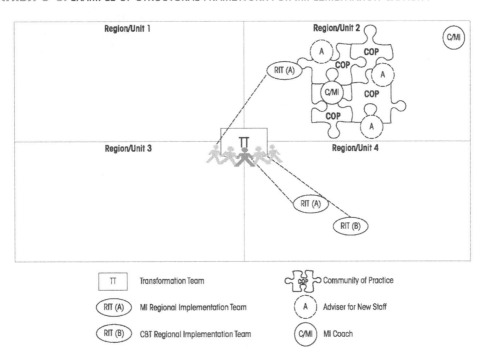

Source: D. Fixsen, K. Blase, R. Homer, and G. Sugai, *Developing the Capacity for Scaling Up the Effective Use of Evidence-Based Programs in State Departments of Education,* Concept Paper (University of North Carolina-Chapel Hill, University of Oregon, and University of Connecticut, 2009).

Conclusion

The reasoning behind the three different strategies for helping staff cultivate MI skills is quite simple. In the first case, with new hires, there is a high-leverage opportunity to expeditiously cultivate strong and positive first impressions about MI and related interpersonal skills. These can potentially go a long way toward establishing and supporting preferred mental models for a learning organization. The second strategy, for staff not yet motivated to learn MI, is a damage control process recommended so that inordinate wastes of resources are avoided. More importantly, it does not create unnecessary and unproductive staff resistance. Finally, working with motivated staff to bring out their skills over time is a high-leverage activity seeking to build a nucleus of MI expertise within the agency in the most efficient and cost-effective way possible. Experience, as well as the body of research in transfer of innovations, suggests that it is far better to propagate a small nucleus of deeper expertise than it is to have a broader first wave transmission that is shallow and lacks real fidelity to the model.

Endnotes

1. S.T. Walters, M.D. Clark, R. Gingerich, and M.L. Meltzer, *Motivating Offenders to Change: A Guide for Probation and Parole* (Washington, DC: U.S. Department of Justice, National Institute of Corrections, 2007).

2. C.E. Yahne, W.R. Miller, T.B. Moyers, and M. Pirritano, *Teaching Motivational Interviewing to Clinicians: A Randomized Trial of Training Methods* (Albuquerque, NM: Center on Alcoholism, Substance Abuse, and Addictions, 2004).

3. W.R. Miller and K.A. Mount, "A Small Study of Training in Motivational Interviewing: Does One Workshop Change Clinician and Client Behavior?" *Behavioural & Cognitive Psychotherapy* 29(4):457–71, 2001.

4. W.R. Miller, T.B. Moyers, L. Arciniega, D. Ernst, and A Forcehimes, "Training, Supervision and Quality Monitoring of the COMBINE Study Behavioral Interventions," *Journal of Studies on Alcohol* 66(4):188–95, 2005.

5. W.R. Miller and S. Rollnick, *Motivational Interviewing: Preparing People for Change,* 2d ed. (New York: Guilford Press, 2002).

6. W.R. Miller and S.R. Rollnick, "The Atmosphere of Change," in *Motivational Interviewing: Preparing People To Change Addictive Behavior* (New York: Guilford Press, 1991), pp. 3–13.

7. M. Lariviere, *Antecedents and Outcome of Correctional Officers' Attitudes Towards Federal Inmates: An Exploration of Person-Organization Fit* (Ottawa, Ontario, Canada: Carleton University, 2001).

8. B. Fulton, A. Stichman, L. Travis, and E. Latessa, "Moderating Probation and Parole Officer Attitudes to Achieve Desired Outcomes," *The Prison Journal* 77(3):295–312, 1997.

9. A.H. Crowe, "Rethinking Probation: Thoughts From a Broader Constituency," *Perspectives* Spring:34–43, 2001.

10. M.K. Harris, *The Goals of Community Sanctions* (Washington, DC: U.S. Department of Justice, National Institute of Corrections, 1986).

11. F. Cullen, J. Cullen, and J. Wozniak, "The Correctional Orientation of Prison Guards: Do Officers Support Rehabilitation?" *Federal Probation* 40:37–44, 1989.

12. K.L. Brown, "Effects of Supervision Philosophy on Intensive Probationers," *Justice Policy Journal* 4(1):2–32, 2007.

13. J.T. Whitehead, *Burnout in Probation and Corrections* (New York: Praeger Publishers, 1989).

14. A.M. Holgate and I.J. Clegg, "The Path to Probation Officer Burnout: New Dogs, Old Tricks," *Journal of Criminal Justice* 19:325–37, 1991.

15. J.T. Whitehead and C.A. Lindquist, "Job Stress and Burnout Among Probation/Parole Officers: Perceptions and Causal Factors," *International Journal of Offender Therapy and Comparative Criminology* 29(2):109–19, 1985.

16. R.A. Shearer, "Strategic Alignment in Community Supervision of Offenders," *Perspectives* Summer:18–21, 2001.

17. K.C. Mena and J.D. Bailey, "The Effects of the Supervisory Working Alliance on Worker Outcomes," *Journal of Social Service Research* 34(1):55–65, 2007.

18. N.C. Jurik and M.I. Musheno, "The Internal Crisis of Corrections: Professionalization and the Work Environment," *Justice Quarterly* 3:457–80, 1986.

19. B.D. Elman and E.T. Dowd, "Correlates of Burnout in Inpatient Substance Abuse Treatment Therapists," *Journal of Addictions and Offender Counseling* 17:56–65, 1997.

20. K.E. Weick, "The Collapse of Sensemaking in Organizations: The Mann Gulch Disaster," *Administrative Science Quarterly* 38(4):628–52, 1993.

21. P.M. Senge, "Personal Mastery: The Spirit of the Learning Organization," in *The Fifth Discipline: The Art & Practice of the Learning Organization* (New York: Doubleday, 1990), pp. 129–62.

22. P.M. Senge, *The Fifth Discipline: The Art & Practice of the Learning Organization* (New York: Doubleday, 1990).

23. R.J. Ohlemiller, "Learning Organizations, 'What Works' and What's Next," *Journal of Community Corrections* 15(1):18–23, 2005.

24. K.S. Cameron, J.E. Dutton, and R.E. Quinn, "Foundations of Positive Organizational Scholarship" in K.S. Cameron, J.E. Dutton, and R.E. Quinn (eds.), *Positive Organizational Scholarship: Foundations of a New Discipline* (San Francisco, CA: Berrett-Koehler, 2003), pp. 3–13.

25. N. Goodloe, "Lessons Learned: Evidence-Based Practices in the Real World," *Perspectives* Winter:33–42, 2009.

26. D.A. Andrews and J. Bonta, *The Psychology of Criminal Conduct,* 4th ed. (Cincinnati, OH: Anderson Publishing, 2006).

27. S. Mohammed and B.C. Dumville, "Team Mental Models in a Team Knowledge Framework: Expanding Theory and Measurement Across Disciplinary Boundaries," *Journal of Organizational Behavior* 22(2):89–106, 2001.

28. N. Park and C.M. Peterson, "Virtues and Organizations," in K.S. Cameron, J.E. Dutton, and R.E. Quinn (eds.), *Positive Organizational Scholarship: Foundations of a New Discipline* (San Francisco, CA: Berrett-Koehler, 2003), pp. 33–47.

29. "Implementing Motivational Interviewing in Correctional Settings: An Interview with Dr. Miller," 2009.

30. R. Zemke, "Systems Thinking," *Training* 38(2):39–46, 2001.

31. L. Tomaino, "The Five Faces of Probation," *Federal Probation* 39(4):42–45, 1975.

32. M.D. Clark, "Entering the Business of Behaviour Change: Motivational Interviewing for Probation Staff," *Perspectives* Winter:39–45, 2006.

33. J.B. Jacobs and E. Olitsky, "Leadership & Correctional Reform," *Pace Law Review* 24(2):447–96, 2004.

34. G.L. May and W.M. Kahnweiler, "The Effect of a Mastery Practice Design on Learning and Transfer in Behavior Modeling Training," *Personnel Psychology* 53:353–73, 2000.

35. M. Hernandez, "Using Logic Models and Program Theory To Build Outcome Accountability,"

Education and Treatment of Children 23(1):24–40, 2000.

36. K. Graham, G.A. Woo, and C. Smythe, *The Evaluation Casebook: Using Evaluation Techniques to Enhance Program Quality in Addictions* (Toronto, Canada: Addiction Research Foundation, 1994).

37. W.K. Kellogg Foundation, *Logic Model Development Guide: Using Logic Models to Bring Together Planning, Evaluation, and Action* (Battle Creek, MI: W.K. Kellogg Foundation, 2004).

38. J. Petersilia, *Evaluating the Performance of Illinois' Spotlight Day Reporting Reentry Centers* (Chicago, IL: Illinois Department of Corrections, 2007).

39. B. Bogue, J. Diebel, and T.P. O'Connor, "Combining Officer Supervision Skills: A New Model for Increasing Success in Community Corrections," *Perspectives* 2(32):30–45, 2008.

40. W.R. Miller and T.B. Moyers, "Eight Stages in Learning Motivational Interviewing," *Journal of Teaching in the Addictions* 5(1):15, 2006.

41. M.B. Madson, A.C. Loignon, and C. Lane, "Training in Motivational Interviewing: A Systematic Review," *Journal of Substance Abuse Treatment* 36(1):101–09, 2009.

42. E. Wenger, *Communities of Practice: Learning, Meaning, and Identity* (New York: Cambridge University Press, 1998).

43. C.D. Norman and T. Huerta, "Knowledge Transfer & Exchange Through Social Networks: Building Foundations for a Community of Practice Within Tobacco Control," *Implementation Science* 1(20), 2006.

44. D.R. Stober, L. Wildflower, and D. Drake, "Evidence-Based Practice: A Potential Approach for Effective Coaching," *International Journal of Evidence Based Coaching and Mentoring* 4(1):1–8, 2006.

45. B. Bogue, *Mentorship* (Washington, DC: U.S. Department of Justice, National Institute of Corrections, 1990), pp. 1–18.

46. T.R. Bacon and K.I. Spear, *Adaptive Coaching: The Art and Practice of a Client-Centered Approach to Performance Improvement* (Mountain View, CA: Davies-Black Publishing, 2003).

47. N. Gehrke, "Toward a Definition of Mentoring," *Theory Into Practice* 27(3):190–94, 1988.

48. R. Pawson, *Mentoring Relationships: An Explanatory Review,* Working Paper 21 (Swindon, Wiltshire: Economic and Social Research Council, UK Centre for Evidence-Based Policy and Practice, 2004).

49. E. Bolton, "A Conceptual Analysis of the Mentor Relationship in the Career Development of Women," *Adult Education* 30(4):195–207, 1980.

50. U.S. General Accounting Office, *Human Capital: Practices That Empowered and Involved Employees* (Washington, DC: U.S. Government Printing Office, 2001).

51. W. Miller, "Pros and Cons: Reflections on Motivational Interviewing in Correctional Settings," *Motivational Interviewing Newsletter: Updates, Education and Training* 6(1):2–3, 1999.

52. P.F. Drucker, *The Executive in Action: Managing for Results Innovation and Entrepreneurship* (New York: HarperCollins Publishers, 1996).

53. P.F. Drucker and J.A. Maciariello, *The Daily Drucker* (New York: HarperCollins Publishers, 2004).

54. D. Fixsen, S.F. Naoom, K.A. Blase, R.M. Friedman, and F. Wallace, *Implementation Research: A Synthesis of the Literature* (Tampa, FL: University of South Florida, Louis de la Parte Florida Mental Health Institute, The National Implementation Research Network, 2005).

55. S. Belenko, H.K. Wexler, and F. Taxman, *Technology Transfer of Evidence-Based Practice (EBP) in Substance Abuse Treatment in Community Corrections Settings* (Washington, DC: U.S. Department of Justice, National Institute of Corrections, 2008).

56. D.D. Simpson, "A Conceptual Framework for Transferring Research to Practice," *Journal of Substance Abuse Treatment* 22(4):171–82, 2002.

57. S.T. Walters, S.A. Matson, J.S. Baer, and D.M. Ziedonis, "Effectiveness of Workshop Training for Psychosocial Addiction Treatments: A Systematic Review," *Journal of Substance Abuse Treatment* 29(4):283–93, 2005.

58. D. Fixsen, K. Blase, R. Homer, and G. Sugai, *Developing the Capacity for Scaling Up the Effective Use of Evidence-Based Programs in State Departments of Education,* Concept Paper (University of North Carolina-Chapel Hill, University of Oregon, and University of Connecticut, 2009).

Glossary

Affirmations	Affirmations are statements that acknowledge and convey respect or appreciation for a client, his/her struggles, and his/her achievements.
Agreement with a twist	A strategy used to respond to resistance, agreement with a twist is a reflection followed by a reframe.
Ambivalence	The coexistence of opposite and conflicting feelings about a given subject, especially as applied to a potential target behavior.
Amplified reflection	A skill used to respond to resistance, amplified reflection reflects back what the person has said, but increases its intensity.
Autonomy	The condition of self-government or independence; the right of everyone to determine his/her own attitude and perspective about a given subject.
Central eight criminogenic needs	The eight dynamic risk factors that have the strongest correlations with recidivism are current dysfunctional family relations, antisocial peer relations, recreation/leisure problems, employment/education problems, alcohol and other drug problems, history of antisocial behavior associated with low self-control problems, antisocial beliefs/attitudes, and criminal personality features.
Change plan	A formal or informal plan for accomplishing a behavioral goal.
Change talk	Self-motivating statements people make that reinforce movement toward a behavior change. Change talk is invariably in relationship to some potential target behavior or problem. There are two stages to change talk: preparatory change talk and mobilizing change talk, which includes commitment language at stronger levels and taking steps, for client speech that refers to new behavior that has recently taken place. There are four subcategories to preparatory change talk that include client statements about: (1) desire for change, (2) ability to change, (3) reasons for change, and (4) need for change. The acronym DARN is used to refer to these different aspects.

Clinical supervision   Clinical supervision is used in counseling, psychotherapy, and other mental health disciplines as well as many other professions engaged in working with people. It consists of the practitioner meeting regularly with another professional, not necessarily more senior, but normally with training in the skills of supervision, to discuss casework and other professional issues in a structured way.

Cognitive-behavioral   Cognition is "the act or process of knowing." Behavior has to do with the way a living being conducts itself or reacts to stimuli. "Cognitive-behavioral" combines the two qualities.

Cognitive-behavioral treatments   Cognitive-behavioral therapy (CBT) is a psychotherapeutic approach; that is, a talking therapy. CBT aims to solve problems concerning dysfunctional emotions, behaviors, and cognitions through a goal-oriented, systematic training process involving skill rehearsals with guided practice.

Coming alongside   A strategy used to respond to resistance, coming alongside allows the agent to acknowledge that the client may indeed decide not to change his/her behavior.

Communities of practice   A formal or informal group that promotes mutual engagement in a joint enterprise with a shared repertoire of skills, tools, and language. A motivational interviewing (MI) community of practice is a group of practitioners that periodically meets together to practice and support each other in their MI skill acquisition.

Contingency management   Contingency management is a type of treatment used in the mental health or substance abuse fields. Patients are rewarded (or, less often, punished) for their behavior (generally, adherence to or failure to adhere to program rules and regulations or their treatment plan).

Decisional-balance work   The process of examining the pros and cons for changing a behavior and the pros and cons for not changing a behavior, in order to become more aware and resolve some of the related ambivalence.

Developing discrepancy   The principle of developing discrepancy recognizes the value of a client's discovering the discrepancy between his/her current behavior pattern and another more preferred pattern. The key to developing discrepancy is trusting and supporting the client in doing his/her own discovery, rather than pointing out and advising him/her on how to discover something that could be meaningful.

Directive	Guiding and providing direction through subtle reinforcements of what the client is saying in a manner that keeps the conversation moving in a direction that helps the client resolve his/her ambivalence to enter into and maintain a change in behavior. Examples of selectively reinforcing client statements are choosing what client content to include in a summary, or deliberately reflecting one side of the client's expressed ambivalence.
Double-sided reflection	A skill used to respond to resistance, double-sided reflection reflects both sides of the ambivalence.
Eight principles for effective interventions	The National Institute of Corrections' model for evidence-based practice principles consists of eight principles organized in sequential order according to how cases are generally managed: (1) assess risk and need with actuarial tools; (2) enhance intrinsic motivation; (3) target interventions according to risk, need, and responsivity principles; (4) skill train with directed practice; (5) increase positive reinforcement; (6) engage ongoing support in the community; (7) measure relevant practices; and (8) provide feedback with positive reinforcement. The model is designed to reinforce differentially directing resources (additive principles) according to the risk of the person being supervised.
Eight principles of evidence-based practice	See "Eight principles for effective interventions."
Eight progressive tasks	See "Eight tasks for learning MI."
Eight tasks for learning MI	According to Moyer and Miller (2006), there are eight tasks involved in learning and mastering an MI style of engaging clients: (1) openness to collaboration with the client's expertise; (2) proficiency in client-centered counseling, including accurate empathy; (3) recognition of key aspects of client speech that guide the practice of MI; (4) eliciting and strengthening client change talk; (5) rolling with resistance; (6) negotiating change plans; (7) consolidating client commitment; and (8) switching flexibly between MI and other intervention styles. There is some supposition that the eight tasks are learned in somewhat sequential order.
Eight-task model	See "Eight tasks for learning MI."
Elaboration	The technique of simply asking to elaborate, once an agent is presenting change talk, is both simple and very effective at the same time. Requests to elaborate can take the form of inquiring about "What else?" or can involve specific requests: "What would a more recent example of that be?" In either case, the goal is to keep the client talking freely in the same vein of change talk.

Eliciting change talk

One of the guiding principles of motivational interviewing is to have the client, rather than the agent, voice the arguments for change. Change talk refers to client statements that indicate a desire, ability, reason, or need for change. The agent can either listen for gratuitous change talk and reinforce it (e.g., ask for elaboration, reflect it, or affirm it) or deliberately elicit it with one of the strategies for eliciting change talk.

Emphasizing personal choice/control

A strategy used to respond to resistance, emphasizing personal choice/control puts the responsibility for change on the client by emphasizing that what the client does is really his/her choice.

Engagement

The level of activation and motivation the client experiences in treatment is positively related to treatment retention and better treatment outcomes in general. Client engagement appears to be a function of client confidence in the treatment, the therapist, or both, and the counselor's personal efficacy and trust for the organization he/she works in. Developing an early working alliance between the client and the counselor is also reported to be a reliable predictor of engagement.

Evidence-based practice

Evidence-based practice (EBP) is the preferential use of mental and behavioral health interventions for which systematic empirical research has provided evidence of statistically significant effectiveness as treatments for specific problems. EBP promotes the collection, interpretation, and integration of valid, important, and applicable client-reported, counselor-observed, and research-derived evidence.

Evocative questions

These are open questions directed at drawing out from the client some aspect of change talk (e.g., desire, ability, reason, or need for change). Some examples are: "What gives you some confidence you could make this change if you decided to?" (ability) or "What about this change do you actually like or look forward to?" (desire).

Experimental/ control research

Research using random assignment of subjects to either experimental or control conditions is considered the gold standard in terms of methodological rigor because the key variable of interest (e.g., intervention X) is absolutely controlled.

Expressing empathy

Expressing empathy is a core principle in motivational interviewing that involves the use of reflective listening skills such as reflections, summaries, open questions, and affirmations, which support a client-centered orientation. Accurate empathy—truly understanding where the other person is coming from moment to moment—is largely a function of expressing empathy.

Far transfer	Both near and far transfer are widely used terms in the training literature. Near transfer refers to transfer of learning when the task and/or context change slightly but remain largely similar. Far transfer refers to the application of learning experiences to related but largely dissimilar problems. For example, transferring the learned performance in the classroom to the workplace represents far transfer.
Goals and values	Engaging clients to look at and draw upon their values can be a very powerful approach for helping people experience a deeper level of discrepancy around their target behavior. This can be done through a card-sort exercise or a discussion of the client's most important values, where the interviewer guides the client into comparing and contrasting how his/her target behaviors match up with his/her values.
Holistic	Relating to or concerned with wholes or with complete systems rather than with the individual parts.
Importance confidence ruler	One of several techniques for deliberately exploring discrepancies the client might be experiencing around a target behavior in a manner that is likely to elicit change talk. The importance confidence ruler approach asks the client to identify (on a 1–10 scale) how important the behavior goal is and then explores why it is not a number somewhat lower than what he/she indicated. The interviewer may also have the client identify a number that represents his/her current confidence for changing the target behavior and then subsequently ask the client what it might take to either increase that confidence number a point or two, or ask what it would take to close the gap between the confidence number and his/her importance ranking (if the latter is the higher of the two).
Intrinsic motivation	Intrinsic motivation refers to motivation that is driven by an interest or enjoyment in the task itself. It exists within the individual rather than relying on any external pressure.
Learning organizations	A learning organization is a group of people working together to collectively enhance their capacities to learn how to create results they really care about.
Listening reflectively	When an agent listens reflectively, he/she emphasizes the use of open questions, affirmations, different kinds of reflections (e.g., simple, double sided, amplified, and other complex reflections), and summaries. This set of client-centered active or reflective listening skills is sometimes referred to by the acronym OARS.

LISTSERV

LISTSERV is currently a commercial product marketed by L-Soft International. Although LISTSERV refers to a specific mailing list server, the term is sometimes used incorrectly to refer to any mailing list server.

Looking back/ Looking forward

This technique is similar to the querying extremes technique for eliciting change talk, insofar as the looking forward component is hypothetical—what might this change enterprise look like if the client stuck with it for a few months?, and/or was there ever a time in the client's life when the target behavior did not exist or was a nonissue, and what did that experience look like for the client as compared to now?

MITI-3

The Motivational Interviewing Treatment Integrity (MITI) 3.1.1 coding instrument is used to measure treatment fidelity for clinical trials of motivational interviewing and is a means of providing structured, formal feedback about ways to improve practice in nonresearch settings.

Motivational Interviewing Skill Code

The Motivational Interviewing Skill Code (MISC) was developed as a method for evaluating the quality of motivational interviewing from audiotapes and videotapes of individual counseling sessions.

Nondirective

Nondirective refers to a willingness to accept and focus on what the client decides to bring up for discussion.

Open questions

Open questions are questions that seek a broad amount of information, allow for a range of possible responses, and convey interest in the client's point of view.

Organizational culture

Organizational culture is the sum total of an organization's past and current assumptions, experiences, philosophy, and values that hold it together; it is expressed in its self-image, inner workings, interactions with the outside world, and future expectations. It is based on shared attitudes, beliefs, customs, express or implied contracts, and written and unwritten rules that the organization develops over time and that have worked well enough to be considered valid. Also called corporate culture, it manifests in (1) the ways in which the organization conducts its business and treats its employees, customers, and the wider community; (2) the extent to which autonomy and freedom are allowed in decisionmaking, developing new ideas, and personal expression; (3) how power and information flow through its hierarchy; and (4) the strength of employee commitment toward collective objectives.

Parallel process
The parallel process is an unconscious replication in the supervisory session of therapeutic difficulties that a supervisee has with a client. This replication may originate with the supervisor unwittingly modeling behavior that is then taken by the social worker into the therapeutic interaction with the client. In this book, the parallel process refers to how the process that is taking place between client and staff can be mirrored in the process between staff and supervisor, and vice versa.

Peer coaching
Peer coaching involves two or more coworkers who work toward a common goal. Coaching sessions can involve refining current practices, building new skills, sharing ideas, or teaching each other different skill sets. This sharing of ideas is used to solve a variety of possible issues in the workplace. Some features of peer coaching are that it is confidential, flexible, and focuses on observable behaviors for generating feedback and providing points of reference.

Querying extremes
Like all of the techniques used for eliciting change talk, querying extremes is used to help clients reexamine their position regarding a particular existing behavior. The interviewer starts by using open questions to learn from the client what it might look like if changing the given behavior were to work out extremely well or, conversely, extremely poorly. Any change talk the client responds with would then be followed up with reflective listening to encourage the client to elaborate, with more change talk.

Randomized clinical trials
Also known as randomized controlled trials, randomized clinical trials are an experimental design used for testing the effectiveness of a new medication or a new therapeutic procedure. Individuals are assigned randomly to a treatment group (experimental therapy) and a control group (placebo or standard therapy) and the outcomes are compared.

RCT research
Research using randomized clinical trials.

Real plays
Real plays, as opposed to role plays, are exercises conducted among peers, where one assumes the role of client and candidly discusses a current personal issue of his/her own so that the partner in the exercise can practice his/her new skills.

Reflections
A reflection is a statement of our hypothesis about what the client is saying. There are three levels to a reflection—repeat, rephrase, paraphrase.

Reframe
A strategy used to respond to resistance, reframes offer a different meaning or interpretation of what the client is saying.

Resistance

Resistance is any observable client behavior that signals the client is becoming uncomfortable with how the conversation is or is not unfolding. Interview styles that confront, challenge, and generally put pressure on the client's ambivalence around changing a behavior frequently result in demonstrations of client resistance.

Retention

Retention refers to the rate at which clients entering a particular treatment condition or program are retained in the program through to the intended final session.

Righting reflex

The righting reflex is a very natural temptation practitioners experience to set a client right or "fix" him/her in some way that the client is fundamentally capable of doing on his/her own. When agents succumb too much to their "righting reflex," they may be inadvertently causing their clients to react negatively (because the client senses that his/her prerogatives are being displaced or diminished). The righting reflex is one of the core principles of motivational interviewing captured in the acronym RULE (resist the righting reflex, understand and explore the person's own motivations, listen with empathy, and empower the client). A strong righting reflex keeps an agent from rolling with resistance, which is another way of stating the same principle.

Rolling with resistance

Rolling with resistance describes the ability to avoid getting "hooked" or caught up in a client's demonstration of resistance, regardless of the form it takes (e.g., rebellious, rationalizing, reluctant, resigned). Rolling with resistance implies taking the client's manifestation of resistance seriously as a signal for changing tactics, but not taking it personally.

Scaffolding

Scaffolding refers to building skills incrementally starting with the most basic elemental version and then moving to more complex or advanced variations of the skill.

Shifting focus

A strategy used to respond to resistance, shifting focus involves bypassing the topic that the client is resisting, rather than confronting it.

Social network enhancement

Social network enhancement interventions are strategies developed to assist clients by improving their existing social support networks. The quality of someone's social support can have a direct as well as a buffering or indirect effect on his/her ability to successfully manage change or achieve his/her goals.

Social support

Social support constitutes the routine, daily interpersonal interactions an individual generally experiences and comes to expect and the degree to which these personal exchanges are positive, fulfilling, and shared with people who the individual can identify with and relate to. The social support or social capital someone has is a significant moderator of treatment outcomes.

Spirit of MI	The spirit of MI (motivational interviewing) is the nontechnical, more adaptive component of MI. There are three components or dimensions to the MI spirit: (1) respect for the other person's autonomy—his/her right to be self-governing and independent of others, (2) interest in evocative methods that empower the client to discover his/her own solutions, and (3) commitment to collaboration with the client as completely as possible. Improvement or growth along these three dimensions implies changing oneself and it is in that sense that the MI spirit is adaptive rather than technical.
Summarizing	A summary is a group of reflections that bring together different aspects of what the client is saying.
Supporting self-efficacy	Supporting self-efficacy is a core principle of motivational interviewing captured in the last letter of the acronym DERS (developing discrepancy, expressing empathy, rolling with resistance, supporting self-efficacy). Supporting self-efficacy means to be willing to pay close attention and either create or use available opportunities for reinforcing the client's sense of capacity or confidence for achieving (prosocial) goals. This principle is also portrayed using the term empower in another acronym (RULE—resist the righting reflex, understand and explore the person's own motivations, listen with empathy, and empower the client) that depicts the same four principles.
Sustain talk	Sustain talk is the language or way that clients talk about a target behavior when they are not really interested in changing it. This disinterest in change is often expressed as desires for status quo, abilities to function with the behavior, reasons that status quo is preferred, and needs for keeping things as they are.
Transformation team	A transformation team performs a state-level coordination function for broadly educating and stimulating project interest, assessing the implementation "evidence" from program developers and purveyors. In addition, the transformation team is responsible for ensuring effective implementation and fidelity, managing scale-up shifts, and coordinating continuous communication regarding the use of implementation drivers on multiple levels.
Working alliance	The working alliance consists of the shared tasks, goals, and bonds between the client and his/her counselor.

U.S. Department of Justice

National Institute of Corrections

Washington, DC 20534

Official Business
Penalty for Private Use $300

Address Service Requested